This is a must-read for every parent. I loved the topics that relate to a specific need and the sweet simple prayers at the end of each chapter. Parenting on Your Knees *is a wonderful book to help moms lighten up, strengthen up, and look up as they embrace their greatest ministry - raising godly children.*

You will find yourself laughing out loud as you identify with what preschoolers say and do. "No Guilt" book - only great empathy, encouragement, understanding, valuable tips/advice, Biblical principles, and simple guidance in prayer as you raise precious little people called - preschoolers.

FERN NICHOLS
President and Founder of Moms in Prayer International

Busy parents will be energized and encouraged as they grow in spiritual wisdom through the dynamic, practical parenting tips. They will immediately connect with Vicki Tiede, who is humorous and has walked her talk. Her fresh, creative ideas to surviving the realities of raising little children are rooted in personalizing prayer! Parenting on Your Knees *will help both parents and children draw from the well of God's grace where obstacles can become opportunities!*

ANNETTA E. DELLINGER
Joyologist, Author-Speaker Joyful Ministries

Parenting On Your Knees

Prayers and Practical Guidance for the Preschool Years

Vicki Tiede

ISBN-13: 978-1-938092-29-9
ISBN-10: 1938092295

Published by Pix-N-Pens Publishing, 130 Prominence Point Pkwy. #130-330,
Canton, GA 30114, www.PixNPens.com

To order additional copies of this resource online, visit www.PixNPens.com.

Printed in the United States of America.

COVER PHOTOS courtesy of Kadi Tiede Photography.
www.KadiTiedePhotography.com.

To my children: Kadi, Ben, and Caleb,
I pray for each of you every day of my life.

Pour out your heart like water
before the presence of the Lord!
Lift your hands to him
for the lives of your children ...

Lamentations 2:19 (ESV)

Table of Contents

Acknowledgements

My most heartfelt appreciation goes to my partner in this parenting adventure, Mike. I thank God for placing you as the head of our home, for giving you wisdom, and for helping you love me as you do.

Kadi, Ben, and Caleb, I pray you all know how deeply you are loved by me, Daddy, and Jesus. Thank you for granting me permission to tell some of our crazy stories in order to encourage other moms and dads. Kadi, thank you also for sharing your gift of photographing newborns and families. I love my cover because my daughter was behind the lens.

Special thanks to my cover models. Scott and Jen, you have been grafted into our family and it only seemed right to have you involved in this journey as you are in the midst of parenting Emily and Jack on your knees.

To the moms who shared your stories with me and trusted me to share them with others – thank you!

Tracy, first I called you friend, then I called you editor, and today I call you my publisher. How sweet is that? I thank God for you.

Above all, I thank my Lord and Savior, Jesus Christ, for calling and permitting me to encourage moms and dads as they embark on parenting on their knees.

Chapter 1

SWEET BLESSINGS

Deciding to Pray for Your Child

And he took the children in his arms, put his hands on them
and blessed them.

Mark 10:16

I remember the exact moment I was presented with my first tiny
bundle of love. A few hours later, the commotion died down, the baby
was clean, calls had been made, and my husband slept in the chair
beside me. Alone at last with this little one, I explored the shape of her
nose, the length of her fingers, and the velvety softness of her skin.
Then I snuggled her up to my heart, and did what seemed natural at the
time, I thanked God and prayed for the sweet blessing in my arms.

When you welcome a new baby into your family, whether by birth
or adoption, something amazing happens. As a parent, you experience
feelings you may have never had before. You sense an urgency to
protect your child and give her everything she needs to thrive and be
happy.

God has blessed you with this little one, to love and care for, but
He wants to share in the joys, hopes, worries, and fears for this child.
He doesn't expect you to travel this road solo. Going to God on behalf
of your child helps you remember you are not parenting alone.

Enjoy the Journey ...

Fast forward a few years, in our home, and add a couple more sweet blessings ...

Like a seasoned pilot my husband ran through his final checklist, "Luggage stowed?"

"Check."

"Snacks?"

"Check."

"House locked?"

"Check."

"Sippy cups and diapers within reach?"

"Check."

"Kids buckled in their seats?"

"Check, check, check!" chorused our three children from their car seats.

They squealed as Daddy backed the minivan out the driveway and announced, "We are cleared for take-off."

Thus began our seven-day car trip with fun stops along the way. However, before we hit the interstate our four-year-old whined, "When're we gonna get there?"

Sticking with his flight theme, my husband answered, "Estimated Time of Arrival for Stop #1 is 12:00."

"How many Veggie Tales is that?" inquired Middle Son.

"Six," I answered.

We were rewarded with a litany of complaints that continued for the duration of the trip. My husband groaned. I prayed. With our children's eyes only on the final destination, I wondered if they would miss all the sweet blessings this journey promised.

> Reserve these moments for time with God.
>
> • Put on quiet worship music.
>
> • Read a short devotional
>
> • Every time you stop to check the clock or burp the baby, take time to thank God for this child and bring your concerns to Him.

If I'm being honest, I can't find fault with the kids just wanting to get there. I do the same thing as a parent. It seems I often have my eyes fixed on the next milestone in my children's lives and I, too, miss the sweet blessings. Sometimes I forget parenting is a process, not an event. It's a journey, not a destination. At the beginning of this parenting trip, I prayed for my baby. If I want to enjoy each side trip along the way, I would do well to remember to stop, drop, and pray … often.

I'm convinced God gives you the early years of your children's lives either to prepare you for their other wild seasons or to give you opportunities to turn your eyes toward Him … or perhaps both. If, like me, you are determined to get the most out of the parenting years, then join me on my knees where we're eye-to-eye with our children and looking up at Jesus, who wants to co-parent with us.

(If you have children under the age of six, and you've managed to capture a few minutes to read this book, congratulations! We have no time to lose though, as I predict you may be interrupted any moment by your little one.)

Making the Decision…

When I held my newborn in my arms and prayed, it seemed like the right thing to do. It was quiet, and the two of us were bonding. I can't say praying for my children has always come that naturally. For one thing, ever since I brought home that first baby, I've not really experienced quiet like that again. Okay, I confess, sometimes they sleep, especially during adolescence, and if I'm not catching up on laundry, loading the dishwasher, or restoring order to my toy-strewn home, I can steal a moment or two of peaceful bliss.

Nevertheless, sometimes praying for my children is a decision more than a heart reflex. I recently heard a riddle that reinforces my point.

Three frogs were sitting on a lily pad. One frog decided to jump. How many frogs were left?

The correct answer is *three*. Remember: *deciding* to jump and *jumping* are two different things. Deciding is a thought. Jumping is an action. Action is what counts!

The same is true when it comes to praying for your children. Deciding to pray and praying are two different things. If you're to enjoy the sweet blessings God has given you to the fullest extent, you need to make the decision to share your children with him in prayer, and then take action.

And whatever you ask in prayer,
you will receive, if you have faith.
Matthew 21:22 (ESV)

Action Plan …

I can almost hear you asking, "Doesn't prayer require a little *quiet* time … alone? Unless I'm in the bathroom (and maybe not then either) I don't get much of that around here."

Parents of young children face interesting challenges to prayer, which are somewhat unique to this season of life. There is nothing quite like the chaos that moves in when you bring that newborn home and attempt to tackle all your responsibilities on less than four hours of sleep. How can someone so small take so much of your time, energy, and focus? You may sit down with a sincere intent to pray, but end up with a stiff neck from an unexpected nap.

Once your children are old enough to don a backpack and climb aboard the big yellow school bus, then parents have plenty of time to pour a cup of coffee and spend time praying and contemplating their current parenting dilemma, right? Not hardly. School years invite new challenges such as carpools, homework to check, forgotten lunches to deliver, room mother responsibilities … You get the picture. Dare we even venture into the season of teenagers and suggest that perhaps *then* you might have oodles of time to sit at Jesus' feet?

The cool thing is that even when you're exhausted, if your heart is open to God, He will find a creative way to speak to you and make His presence known. You may hear His voice in the middle of the night, in a silly thing your child says, in a song you hear on the radio or in a gentle touch or look from your child.

I remember sitting and rocking the baby for a late night feeding and thinking how peaceful it was. During the first few months when he was up a lot, I was often too wiped out to appreciate those precious moments. In time, I figured out that those middle of the night meetings provided me with a special opportunity to pray for my baby.

Fast forward to the teen years and again you find yourself hooting with the owls while you wait for your child to get home from a job or a date before curfew.

A Season …

For everything there is a season, and children have many seasons as they grow and change. Sleep patterns, eating schedules, socialization and personality development all change, sometimes daily, it seems. Parents are hard pressed to keep up with the changes and can often feel overwhelmed. The household begins to revolve around the child's schedule. You long for a routine. When one is finally established, you'll have time to pray, right? Not necessarily.

When my third child settled into a schedule, I remember celebrating. For a while, I filled my new *free* time with an endless parade of "shoulds" which clamored for my attention: laundry, dishes, bill paying, meal planning ... Prayer seemed to slip down the list, sometimes dropping out of sight.

Then a wise friend advised me that I was too busy ***not*** to pray. I needed to make it a practice to feed my spirit during those brief breaks, which helped me be more productive in the long run. I'm going to step into the shoes of my sage friend and pass on her wisdom to you. ***You*** are also too busy not to pray, and you'll never have another chance to pray for your child at this point in their development.

God has provided a way for you to enjoy this unique season of parenting children from birth to eighteen. He wants you to enjoy the sweet blessings of your kids and the precious moments you will experience during these years. It happens when you decide to parent your children on your knees. Don't just decide to start praying ... Jump off that lily pad.

Chapter Two
PARENTING PRESCHOOLERS ON YOUR KNEES
Beginning to Pray for Your Little One

For this child I prayed, and the Lord has granted me my petition
that I made to him.
Therefore I have lent him to the Lord.
As long as he lives, he is lent to the Lord.
1 Samuel 1:27-29 (ESV)

When the pacifier goes AWOL, you can tuck your pinkie knuckle into your baby's mouth and quiet his screams. A superhero is born as soon as a dishtowel is tied around a neck and a wooden spoon is wielded. And vegetables are munched when laid out in smiley faces. Call it desperation or Creative Parenting 101, either way … it works.

As a parent of young children, you may not pray by conventional means either. Your prayer time may look quite different than it does for your friends who have no children, school-aged children, or grown children. God loves parents of preschoolers, and he desires to spend time with you, even if it's in unusual or creative ways. John Eldredge affirms this idea in *Wild at Heart*:

"Time with God is not about academic study or getting through a certain amount of Scripture or any of that. It's about connecting with God. We've got to keep those lines of communication open, so use whatever helps. Sometimes I'll listen to music; other times I'll read Scripture or a passage from a book; often I will journal; maybe I'll go for a run; then there are days when all I need is silence and solitude and the rising sun. The point is simply to do whatever brings me back to my heart and the heart of God."

While you wipe another nose, take your toddler to the bathroom, and rock a little one to sleep you long to spend time with God. To make such a meeting possible, you must take some creative action.

- When you pay your electric bills, pray that your children will know Jesus as the Light of the world.
- When you see a school bus, pray that your children will learn new skills and strive toward greater achievements.
- When you water your plants, pray that your children will grow healthy and strong.

Create Reminders …

As you go through your days, constant reminders taunt your senses of all you need to do. You see the dishes stacked on the counter, smell the diapers that need to be taken outside, and hear your children whining for dinner. Prayer can have physical reminders too.

Write Verses …

You can be encouraged by God's truths when you write out verses that speak to your heart and place them in strategic places. This way you can single out a few moments and put all of your energy into a verse.

Try taping verses on the:
- Changing table
- High chair
- Bathroom mirror
- Dashboard of the car/minivan
- Arm of the rocking chair where you rock and feed your baby

Redefine "Quiet Time"…

Quiet time alone with the Lord looks very different during this season of life. There is little opportunity to sit down and focus exclusively on spending uninterrupted time with God.

Hide …

At the end of the day, when I finally have everyone tucked in bed and the house is quiet, I may sit down and plan to spend time in prayer and quiet Bible study. ("Quiet" being the operative word.) However, more often than not, my mind wanders to the dishes that aren't washed yet, the laundry still piled on the floor, and the toys scattered around the family room. That's when I need to go to my closet to pray. *But you, when you pray, go into your inner room, close your door and*

As parents of little ones, you can do things such as:
- Listen to worship music while playing with your children
- Pray in the car or shower
- Read Bible stories with your tots
- Listen to God in the middle of the night when you are up for a feeding

pray to your Father who is in secret, and your Father who sees what is done in secret will reward you (Matthew 6:6 NASB).

I have been known to hide in my walk-in-closet, on occasion, even when the kids aren't sleeping. Sometimes I require a "Mommy time out" for a few minutes. In those instances, I'm often doing some deep breathing or shooting arrow prayers to Jesus.

Shoot Arrow Prayers…

Like an arrow shooting directly to heaven, "arrow prayers" are short, quick prayers you send straight to God. These prayers can come at any time and in any place. They are especially handy when you don't have time for a lengthy, formal prayer, but you need instant "action" from God.

- *Hide in the bathroom, closet, garage, or any out of the way space*

- *Set a timer for the first few minutes of naptime for prayer*

- *Give yourself permission to take a five minute break from chores to pray*

When my three-year-old "flew" off his bed like Superman, and took a gash out of his side, I shot up, "Lord, please let Ben not have a broken bone." Losing my toddler at a department store required firing off, "Father, please keep Caleb safe and me calm!" When dangers pop up unexpectedly in your life, and there is no time to take a knee in prayer, arrow prayers serve as your cry for God's intervention.

Parents of preschoolers tend to depend on arrow prayers for many other purposes as well. You shoot prayers of thanksgiving when your preschooler indicates, for the first time, she needs to use the potty. Ah, the end of expensive diapers is in sight. You dispatch praise to Jesus when your spouse comes home from work or grandma calls and offers to take the kids, just when mommy needs a break.

Mommies and Daddies also fling requests for assistance when life's little irritants get the best of us, "God, can you please help me find my car keys?" Sometimes it's advantageous to pray these arrow prayers out loud for little ears to hear, "Jesus, please help Kadi remember I love her and that you want her to obey me." It never hurts for your children to realize you're taking your needs straight to the top!

Get Spiritual Nutrition...

Arrow prayers have special value in the life of a parent of preschoolers, but your daily spiritual nutrition needs to include more than that. In a pinch, you could feed your little ones Cheerios for breakfast, lunch, and dinner. If this were your practice every day, however, not only would they complain loud and long, their health would be jeopardized. Likewise, you need more than quick conversations with Jesus for your spiritual health. You need some meat.

* *Read some portion of God's Word daily. (Even if it's one verse.)*
* *Meditate on what you've read while doing chores.*
* *Keep this book or another devotional or prayer book someplace you spend time each day - like the bathroom.*
* *Keep a list of prayer requests over the sink, over the changing table, or anywhere that will catch your eye.*
* *Join a local support/fellowship group for parents of young children. Be involved in the lives of others and lift them in prayer.*

Establish Realistic Expectations...

"For I know the plans I have for you," declares the LORD
(Jeremiah 29:11).

That's right. He has a plan for you and for your children. He planned for this preschool season. He also planned for good parenting days and bad parenting days. You can rest in knowing that even on your worst parenting days He is working His plan for good in your life and in the lives of your children. Whew! What a relief!

God also planned for those days when your house full of preschoolers feels like a chaotic jungle full of prowling tigers ready to pounce. He knew that on those days you might only be able to snatch brief moments with Him, mostly in the form of "S.O.S." prayers! But guess what? He's not keeping track.

You don't get a better address in heaven if you spend bigger chunks of time with Him and neglect your responsibilities. Are you setting your "quiet time" standard too high in order to keep up with what you think the other parents at church, on the cul-de-sac, or at the park are doing? I hope not. Instead, you should be setting realistic expectations and embrace the time you have with God, great or small, for the purpose of pleasing Him and igniting a desire to pray.

Just as you long to have your children climb up in your lap and lay their head against your heart, Jesus wants you to come to Him for moments of tenderness. He isn't concerned if you climb off His lap after a short time because you are needed by your little ones. Your time with Him, no matter how it looks to you, is as precious to Him as crayon masterpieces drawn by your preschoolers. They still earn a place on the refrigerator because they're valuable treasures. Your prayers, no matter how small, delight Jesus and earn a space on His "refrigerator." Our creativity needs to be channeled into finding ways to spend moments with Him.

Be Proactive...

If you take steps to prepare your children when you want to have quiet time, then you might just pull it off without too many interruptions. Begin by telling them Mommy or Daddy needs to spend some time with Jesus on the couch every day.

When you take your Bible to the couch, set the timer for a few minutes. Tell the children they need to try not to interrupt until the timer rings. In the beginning, I could only set the timer for 3 minutes, but I built on that time each day. Try getting a special timer for "Mommy and Daddy's Time with Jesus." Most importantly, plan something for the children to do that they don't normally get to do. They'll look forward to your quiet time too. A special busy box can be a huge hit with little ones.

Take a Knee ...

Despite the challenges you face, the time to start praying for your little ones is *now*, from the time they are born and forever after. We are all helpless and needy when it comes to asking Jesus for the things we need, but none more so than young children. As parents, we are better equipped to pray on behalf of our young children than anyone else.

In the early years of your parenting joyride, you may make frequent stops and starts, bumble over bumps in the road, and change directions many times, but none of that will deter you from your destination. When you pray for your little one's character, development, social skills, behavior, and spiritual growth, you will enjoy the sweet blessings of parenting on your knees.

Delight yourself in the Lord,
and he will give you the desires of your heart.
Psalm 37:4

Praying for Your Little One's Character

Chapter Three
I "FINK" I CAN
Praying for Your Little One to Persevere

I wasn't prepared for the pain my heart would feel watching my middle child learn to speak. When Ben was two and a half, my mommy heart told me his speech development was not where it should have been. A trip to a respected speech therapist at the Mayo Clinic confirmed what my heart had already known. Ben had a significant speech disorder.

Thus began our experience with therapy. Two to three times a week for a year, we made time in our life for speech therapy. By the second year, we graduated to once a week. Throughout this experience, Ben has been an amazing little trooper! I can't explain how proud we are of his progress, which was born from his perseverance.

Time and time again we correct Ben's speech in the course of a day, modeling correct pronunciation for him. He asks for a treat by saying, "I can have a granola bar?" and we correct, "*Can* I have a granola bar?" Patiently he fixes his error. We ask him which kind he would like to have and he says, "I yust want whis one." Again, we model, "I *just* want *this* one. Stick out your tongue, buddy." He tries again, sometimes multiple times. Successful, he takes his granola bar and off he goes, never complaining, never getting frustrated with our interruptions, and never giving up.

Ben has learned a great deal about correct speech from his lessons, but he has unwittingly taught us even more. He has taught us to persevere, to never give up no matter how difficult the climb to the top. To quote my precious son as he retells the story of <u>The Little Engine that Could</u>, "I fink I can." You'd better believe it! He does.

And let us not grow weary of doing good,
for in due season we will reap, if we do not give up.
Galatians 6:9

Persevere is such a great word! The prefix "per" means to go through something. The root "severe" refers to something that causes distress or difficulty. Sometimes in life we have no choice but to persevere. We have to keep on going, even if the road is rough and seems endless.

It can be difficult to watch our children experience circumstances that require their perseverance. Our little ones have to persevere as they learn many of their life skills. Toddling about on their little legs for the first time requires perseverance. They take a step, flap their little arms for balance, and fall down. Then they roll forward to their knees, push themselves up, struggle for balance, and attempt another step. This is perseverance in action.

As parents, we want to run to their rescue. We anticipate their frustration as their wobbly legs fail them, and we long to come to their aid. Stepping in eliminates their momentary anxiety, but it does nothing to teach perseverance or skills that will be necessary as they mature. Instead, we need to set realistic expectations for our preschoolers and allow them to learn skills through their trials and errors. Then we need to focus our attention more on their effort and less on their performance. Celebrate their stick-to-it-iveness with enthusiasm!

We all have mountains to conquer. The goal isn't to be the first one to the summit. Rather, the goal for our little ones is to keep moving, for we "press on toward the goal for the prize of the upward call of God in Christ Jesus" (Philippians 3:14). Our preschoolers need to keep on keeping on to become all God has planned for them.

And so I pray…

Dear Faithful God, It is so awesome to know that nothing I do is accomplished without you! You are worthy! Holy! Mighty! Yes! Lord, sometimes I'd rather give up than continue on toward my goal. What kind of example am I for _____? Please teach me your ways. Encourage my child as he perseveres through the challenges that come his way. Thank you for seeing the greatest potential for _____. Show him how he may give you his best! I rejoice in the challenges you place in _____'s path because I know it *"produces perseverance; perseverance, character; and character, hope. And hope does not disappoint us"* (Romans 5:4-5 NIV). Amen.

My Personal Prayer:

How God Answered My Prayer:

Children's Book:

Keep Trying Travis by Happy Day Book

Parenting Resource:

Complete Book of Baby & Child Care: From Pre-Birth through the Teen Years by Dr. Paul Reisser and Dr. James Dobson

Chapter Four
THE "TENAMENMENTS"
Praying for Your Little One to Grow in Wisdom

When the Sunday School Director taught all of the kids in church the song, "God's Top Ten," she had no idea the four-year-olds would become little ambassadors of truth at every opportunity. And then the moms of these "Commandment police" began sharing their stories.

Deepali's Mom ~ "I recently took away a ball over which Deepali and her big sister, Abby, were fighting. In our home the policy is, 'If you can't share it, it belongs to Mommy.' This particular day, I owned a ball. Deepali wisely waited until the next day to approach me with her concern about my actions. She counseled, 'Mommy, you shouldn't have taken our ball yesterday because you didn't obey Number 8' (the eighth Commandment prohibiting stealing)."

Drew's Mom ~ "Drew started out playing nicely with his baby sister, but before long he was pulling on Callan's leg. I stopped him, but soon he was at it again. Exasperated, I explained that when he disobeyed me, he also disobeyed God. I reminded him of the fifth Commandment, which instructs children to honor their parents. I added that honoring means obeying. Drew seemed to ponder this for a short time and then threw in his own wisdom concerning God's Word, "But Mom, the Commandments don't say, 'You should not PULL!'"

Ben's Mom (That's me!) ~ "My husband was recently teasing our oldest daughter. Wielding her coveted bag of Hot Cheetos in his hand, he threatened to throw them at her. After she cautioned him that the bag was open and throwing it would result in a big mess, he changed tactics and said he'd just keep them and eat them himself. Four-year-old Ben was sitting in the middle of this exchange, taking it all in. He could remain silent no longer. 'That is a Tenamenment!' he announced with confidence. My husband looked confused, and I started to giggle.

'He means a Ten Commandment,' I whispered.

Then Ben added, 'I think it's number five!' Not quite, but then, a little knowledge can be a dangerous thing."

If any of you lacks wisdom, let him ask God,
who gives generously to all without reproach,
and it will be given him.
James 1:5

Wisdom is a loaded word. According to Webster, it means, "having or showing good judgment and following the best course of action, based on knowledge, experience, and understanding." Wow! This sounds like an impossible bar to jump for a preschooler. As parents, we want our little ones to grow in wisdom. But, sorry to say, it doesn't happen overnight.

When our preschooler ignores our warning about touching the casserole dish that just came out of the oven, she understands and becomes wise. When we caution our child about jumping off stairs and he crashes his head into the wall when his loss of balance propels him forward, he understands and becomes wise. Sometimes lessons are painful, but not always.

Feeding smooshed vegetables to an infant is not always met with favorable results in the beginning. However, as we expose our little connoisseur to vegetables day after day, in time she will learn to, if not enjoy at least tolerate, this particular food group. Learning to walk, climb stairs, even manipulate caregivers, are skills and behaviors, which are learned by repeated exposures. Experience is a great teacher and will help our child grow in wisdom.

Have you seen the illustration of a child's head with the top of it flipped open like the lid of a hinged box? All kinds of things are being poured into this open cavity. This picture provides a great image of how our children are hungry for knowledge and capable of more than we can imagine. As parents, we need to make sure that there is more 'good' stuff being poured in than 'bad' stuff. When our children are little we need to start reading quality books to them every single day. Use daily routines as teachable moments; counting spoons as they place them on the table, or drawing shapes in the driveway with sidewalk chalk. Explain how things work and why you do the things you do, as you go about your day. Most importantly, play, play, play! Acquiring knowledge for preschoolers is supposed to be fun.

The entire book of Proverbs extols the benefits of wisdom. As children mature and grow in their understanding, experiences, and knowledge, they should also be hearing about God's commands, love, and faithfulness. Helping our children grow spiritually wise will equip them to understand and apply the instruction of Proverbs 3:5-6, *"Trust in the Lord with all your heart and do not lean on your own understanding. In all your ways acknowledge him, and he will make straight your paths."*

And so I pray…

Dear Teacher, You are faithful to show us your ways and write your Word on our hearts. I admit that I don't always remember your teachings, and every day I blow it. Thrill me with your Word and give me a hunger for knowledge that comes only from you. Show me how to share that knowledge with _____ . Fill my little one with wisdom as he grows so your teachings may prolong his life for many years. May wisdom and discernment keep him safe. May his foot not stumble on life's rough roads. Jesus, please help _____ not forget your teachings …keep your commandments in his heart, and …let love and faithfulness never leave…so he may win favor and a good name in the sight of you and man (Proverbs 3). Amen.

My Personal Prayer:

How God Answered My Prayer:

Children's Books:

God's Wisdom for Little Girls by Elizabeth George

God's Wisdom for Little Boys by Jim George

Parenting Resource:

Don't Make me Count to Three by Ginger Plowman

Chapter Five

PASSION FOR PATIENCE

Praying for Your Little One to Have Patience

It was that time of day, not long since snack and too long until dinner, when Amanda, a three-year-old drama queen, lamented that she could not possibly wait another moment for dinner. They were having her favorite meal that night, spaghetti. Scooping Amanda up into her arms, her mother snuggled with her on the couch and attempted to explain patience to her little one. "Amanda, patience is waiting – with no whimpering, no whining, and no wailing."

The wheels were turning in that little head covered with thick dark curls. "Do I have to be patient forever and ever?" she wondered out loud.

"No, Amanda," her mother assured her, "but always longer than we would like."

Amanda ran off to her room, and her mother supposed she was trying to find a way to pass time until she could enjoy her dinner. But soon, too soon, came the sound of whimpering…then whining…and finally, wailing. Lots of wailing! Making her way to Amanda's bedroom, Mom found her sitting on her bed, surrounded by every stuffed animal she owned. Seeing her mom in the doorway she ran to her and cried, "Mommy, I passion! I passion!" "Yes, Amanda, you do have passion. THAT you understand! We'll work on patience another day."

...be patient with everyone.

1 Thessalonians 5:14

I would love to find a book entitled, "How to Teach Your Child Patience When You Have Lost Your Own." Can you relate? Patience is not an easy thing to teach, especially when you struggle with it yourself. I don't know about you, but I don't even buy green bananas, because I can't wait for them to ripen enough to be enjoyed as they should be. In this computerized, digitized, mechanized world we live in, we are continuously being offered "new, improved, and faster" ways to accomplish things. Consequently, as children and adults we become paralyzed by impatience when we occasionally have to ... hold your breath ... wait.

Despite the difficulty of teaching patience, it is necessary. Children are naturally self-centered, believing the entire world revolves them and we parents exist to meet their demands and desires immediately. Patience seems to fall on a continuum. As a newborn, we don't expect our child to exercise much patience. His needs are entirely dependent on his caregivers, so he cries and generally we respond quickly. As our little ones grow, they become more independent and their need for instant gratification is more reflective of their desire than need. They WANT a cookie right now, they don't NEED a cookie right now ... although your two-year-old might beg to differ. As they move along the continuum, the hope is that they also learn more patience.

Understanding that they live in an imperfect world with imperfect people and will sometimes have to wait comes as our preschoolers mature. The truth of the matter is things are not always going to go the way they would like. So we teach our children that sometimes they have to "wait without whimpering, whining, and wailing."

Role-play situations in which your children might need to interrupt a conversation or phone call, teaching them when it is acceptable and how to do so politely. Have special things ready for your children to enjoy for those moments when you know their patience is going to be stretched. Several years ago a character on a TV program used to say, "Put your finger on your nose, and count to eight while you wait." Our family has used that phrase and technique many times with our children and, yes, people do look at them a little funny, but at least they aren't whimpering, whining, and wailing while they count. Most importantly, we reward them with high praise when they exercise patience quietly. Patience proves to be a kinder, gentler way to *"bear with one another in love"* (Ephesians 4:2).

And so I pray…

Dear Jesus, You are patient when I am not. Thank you. Thank you. I don't even have to tell you all the times I am impatient with my child, the woman sitting at the green light talking on her cell phone, or anything else that doesn't operate on my time schedule. Forgive me for not waiting without whining. Please help my little one develop patience too. _____ doesn't like to wait for anything. Help me see the ways she is making efforts and remind me to praise her for her successes. Help _____ learn that the world doesn't always revolve around her and that she will be blessed with sweet rewards for waiting for your perfect timing. Amen.

My Personal Prayer:

How God Answered My Prayer:

Children's Book:

Remy the Rhino Learns Patience by Andy McGuire

Parenting Resource:

Creative Correction: Extraordinary Ideas for Everyday Discipline by Lisa Welchel

Chapter Six
THE GREAT TARGET TACKLE
Praying for Preschooler and Self-Control

It was a big step for her husband, Peter, when James, their youngest, was old enough for Cubbies Club at AWANA. Peter had been helping with this program for kids at the church for many years. Their oldest, Heather, was in Sparks, in first grade, and she and Daddy had been going to AWANA for a few years together. When James turned three, he was old enough to go too. This posed a big challenge for Daddy, who had never up to that point taken both the children out of the house on his own.

Things went well the first few weeks. Then one night, Peter said to his wife, "Honey, we will be a little late coming home because Target has jeans on sale. I'm going to stop and pick up a couple of pairs on the way home."

Since she wasn't expecting them at the usual time, she didn't think anything out of the ordinary had occurred when they were 30 minutes past the regular "come home" time.

When they walked in, James was tear-streaked, Heather was wide-eyed, and Peter was tight-lipped. "Later," was all he said as they prepared the kids for bed. Then he told her the story of "The Great Target Tackle."

Peter had made the tactical error of not putting James in a shopping cart. This had never happened in James' young life, being allowed to walk in a store the size of Target. New and wonderful worlds unfolded before his eyes as he surveyed the clothing racks from his 30-inch viewpoint. When Peter stopped to look at the jeans, James darted in, under, and around the racks, giggling wildly.

When told to "Come here, James," he darted farther into the world of fabric and hiding places.

"I couldn't catch him!" Peter was so exasperated. His supportive wife was trying not to laugh, knowing Peter wouldn't appreciate it.

"Whatever did you do?" Secretly she was thinking, "See, buddy, it ain't so easy, is it? Think about this the next time you hand me a list of errands to run when I have both the children with me." Not very charitable on her part, but, hey, she's human.

Peter resumed his story. "I chased him through the men's section, the boy's section, and right into the women's lingerie. He is really fast!"

By this time, she was giggling and he was glaring. "I sent Heather around one side of a rack of nightgowns, and I went the other way. Then Heather shouted, "There he is, Daddy!" James was running down the aisle for all he was worth, headed straight for the front doors."

She was dying at this point. She could see it all unfolding before her. She knew she would need to sober up and take a hard look at her son's scandalous behavior, but at the moment it was all playing rather comically for her.

"Heather took off after him, and tackled him about ten feet from the registers. She sat on him, while he howled away, until I could get there. There we were in our AWANA uniforms, James pinned and yowling, Heather sitting and scowling, and me striding toward them thinking, 'I will never take them anywhere again!'"

Peter didn't get his jeans that night. He didn't take both children into a store by himself again for a long time either.

For this is the will of God, that each one of you know how to control his own body in holiness and honor…
1 Thessalonians 4:3-4

When we bring our precious bundles home from the hospital, their little heads bobble around without proper support, they wet everything in sight each time the diaper comes off, and they spit up with no warning. They define "lack of self-control." Time passes, muscles strengthen, coordination improves and soon they are looking around with nary a dip of the head, and the lucky soul changing the diaper doesn't need to wear a wetsuit to get the job done. With each new milestone in your little one's life she adds a fragment of self-control to her repertoire. She learns to walk without wobbling and controls the urge to potty until she reaches the toilet.

Once our children learn to have self-control over their bodies, it is time to teach them to have self-control over their emotions, thoughts, behaviors, and words. As parents we want our children to express their feelings appropriately and choose to think positively instead of negatively. Our children demonstrate self-control when they are able to sit without wiggling when necessary, and to wisely consider their words before blurting out an insult toward their sibling.

We encourage self-control when we model it ourselves. What our children learn in our homes is more often caught than taught. If we demonstrate lack of self-control in our own lives, it is likely that our children will follow our example. On the other hand, if as parents, we treat others with kindness and respect and we exercise self-control as we navigate our daily lives, we are modeling a standard worthy of replication. We need to begin teaching self-control early, while our children are toddlers. It is much easier to deal with a three-year-old who is learning to control his quick tongue, than a thirteen-year-old who is talking back.

Parents also need to establish reasonable expectations that are high, but attainable, and explain them to our children before they need to be implemented. For instance, consider James and the "Great Target Tackle." James exhibited a total lack of self-control. He had decided that the world of naughtiness beckoned and all ties to obedience must be cut forthwith. His parents may laugh about it now, but they learned quickly that James needed to be taken in hand and taught some self-control. Telling James exactly what behavior was expected of him, BEFORE entering the store may have eliminated this Target trauma.

As parents, we want our young children to learn self-control so life will go well for them as they grow-up. When children are able to exercise self-control they begin to think maturely about their choices and decide to serve others and demonstrate the love of God.

And so I pray….

Father God, I praise you for your love, which is unending. I confess that as a parent I am not always the best example of self-control. Sometimes I eat things, watch things, do things, and say things that are not pleasing to you. Help me model self-control for my little one. Cause _____ to "make every effort to supplement his faith with virtue, and virtue with knowledge, and knowledge with self-control, and self-control with steadfastness, and steadfastness with godliness, and godliness with brotherly affection, and brotherly affection with love. For if these qualities are (his) and are increasing measure, they keep him from being ineffective or fruitful in the knowledge of our Lord Jesus Christ" (2 Peter 1:5-8). Amen.

My Personal Prayer:

How God Answered My Prayer:

Children's Book:

Play with Me by Marie Hall Ets

Parenting Resource:

Don't Make me Count to Three by Ginger Plowman

Chapter Seven

A DIRTY JOB

Praying for Your Little One to Learn Responsibility

Benjamin loved being a big brother and his mother's helper. He fetched burp rags, manned the baby monitor, and was rewarded with silly grins from his baby brother when he made outrageous faces. When baby James was 10 months old, Benjamin decided he was ready to tackle diapers. His mother wondered if he was taking his big brother responsibilities to an extreme. However, not wanting to discourage his "helpfulness," his mom included him on a few routine wet diaper changes. She provided a running commentary, describing the process of removing the soiled diaper, cleaning the baby, and securing the new diaper in place.

One morning, Benjamin's mom was on the telephone when she heard the telltale wails of her youngest son waking from his nap. Because she was tethered to the wall by the phone cord, there was no way to retrieve him from his crib at the moment. He would have to wait until she could end the conversation. In no time, James was quiet again. Assuming he had gone back to sleep, she continued her phone call.

Several minutes had passed when five-year-old Benjamin proudly marched into the kitchen. Beaming, he announced, "I just changed a DIRTY diaper!" Surely he didn't say "dirty" his mother reasoned as she followed her young custodian back to the place of conquest? Sure enough! A brief whiff of the air and a cursory glance at the mess on the floor confirmed that Benjamin had indeed taken care of his brother's "business." James now sat chewing on a sock he had rescued from his right foot, his diaper only slightly askew, while Benjamin burst buttons on his bibbies at the pride he felt by his accomplishment.

For each will have to bear his own load.
Galatians 6:5

When our children are hungry, we feed them. When they are falling asleep on our lap, we put them to bed. When they want a hug, we snuggle them in our arms. When they want to help sweep the kitchen floor, we tell them they are too little. WHAT? It sounds crazy when it's put that way, but it's true. Preschoolers love to help and too often, in our busyness or desire for quality, we tell them they are too young. We must STOP THIS INSANITY! If our little ones want to help around the house, give that peanut a broom, dust clothe, and laundry basket! Hallelujah!

Our family has discovered that when we have long-term guests or frequent visitors to our home, they feel more comfortable and accepted when we include them in daily chores. The same is true of our children. Sadly, in this age of smaller families and more conveniences, such as dishwashers and clothes dryers, children are being assigned fewer and fewer responsibilities. Children, however, need to have responsibilities in order to feel like valuable and appreciated members of the family. Our family embraces the acronym for TEAM that suggests that Together Each Accomplishes More. When every member of Team Tiede contributes to the family jobs, we operate more efficiently.

Learning to be responsible is a process that starts early. When our toddler expresses a desire to help, we need to respond appropriately. So what if the table looks like it was set by a two-year-old? It WAS set by a two-year-old! In fact, maybe we could learn something from them? Our youngest child often set the napkins on the chairs and a handful of forks and spoons at each place at the table. This makes complete sense if you consider that we want our children to keep their napkins in their laps and with young children, forks and spoons are frequently being dropped on the floor and replacements are needed. Our way is not always the best way.

When we respond to the natural desires of our children to learn responsibility, and we instruct and encourage them even when the desire is not there, we will see our little ones grow in confidence and ability. This responsibility will translate into a servant's heart as they grow into adulthood, serving others and serving Jesus.

And so I pray…

Gracious God, You are worthy of all my praise! Glory to you and all you do! I'm sorry that I don't always model responsibility for my child like I should. I know the things that need to be done, and I don't do them. Forgive me for giving my little one the wrong message. Help me teach _____ to learn and embrace responsibility. Give me the words of encouragement that will sing in his heart, and keep me from using words of criticism. Fill _____ with a desire to help in our home and to do so with a right attitude. As _____ becomes more competent, may he grow in confidence and desire to serve you. Amen.

My Personal Prayer:

How God Answered My Prayer:

Children's Book:

> *Zachary's Zoo* by Mike and Amy Nappa

Parenting Resource:

> *Don't Make me Count to Three* by Ginger Plowman

Chapter Eight
THE TEACHER'S SON
Praying for Your Little One and Respecting Authority

During the school year, Evan's daddy sells pop to the students in the school where he teaches. One warm spring day his mommy was delivering a load of pop to school. Not wanting to wake her napping baby, she turned to her oldest son, then almost four years old. "Evan," she instructed, "Please go in and tell Daddy that we need four big kids to come out and help us carry in this load of pop." Eager to be given such an important responsibility, he climbed out of the minivan and ran into the school building.

Evan navigated the familiar route to his Daddy's classroom. When he went into the study hall full of seventh through twelfth graders he looked around, but didn't see Daddy. Evan stepped back into the hall. He paused to consider his options. Remembering that Mommy had given him an important job to do, he decided to complete the mission with or without Daddy! Evan confidently marched back into the classroom and announced in his biggest, most authoritative voice, "I need four guys to carry pop. Who wants to help?"

The high-schoolers looked back and forth at each other. Unsure whether this three year old was here on his own or whether he was an ambassador for his father, their teacher, the boys began raising their hands. Evan chose four young men and led them out to the waiting van.

Unaware of the scene that had just taken place inside the school; Evan's mommy passed a case of pop to the arms of a teenager. It was then that she noticed a familiar figure coming out of an adjacent building. It was her husband! Hadn't he just sent out these students to help her? After conducting a brief interrogation of the high school students and Evan, the real story unfolded. Evan's parents marveled at the authority their son had simply because he represented his father.

Children, obey your parents in the Lord, for this is right.
"Honor your father and mother"
—this is the first commandment with a promise—
"that it may go well with you and that you may live long in the land."
Ephesians 6:1-3

This Bible verse is the bottom line. Some people may consider it strange to *demand* that children respect and honor their parents. However, when children learn to respect their Mommy and Daddy, they ultimately learn to respect God as their heavenly parent as well.

Our little ones are like flawless mirrors, reflecting every strength and imperfection in our parenting. As parents, if we speak disrespectfully to our spouse, our children, or our own parents, we are providing a very poor example. Our speech isn't the only demonstration of respect either. Do we show respect to others in our actions or the way we talk about those people in front of our children? Our preschoolers are always watching.

Other children also influence preschoolers. Many of us have experienced spending time with family friends who allow their children to speak and behave disrespectfully toward their parents. When this happens, it is very important to discuss this with your children when your family is alone. Such a discussion might include asking your child if they noticed how their friend spoke to his daddy. Then you can discuss why that was wrong and what the consequence would be if your child ever copied that behavior.

Television is another destructive influence. Our family has had to seriously limit the television programs that we allow our little ones to watch. Take the time to watch some of your children's programs with them and carefully look for common themes and behaviors of their characters. We found that many popular programs aimed at children boast little ones' sassing, putting down, and lying to their parents. Disrespect is rampant.

There are currently several reality programs on television, which feature extremely naughty and disrespectful children who are then corrected by a "child-rearing expert." Young viewers are not always able to discern the fact that the behavior they are seeing is grossly unacceptable and it can quickly be imitated. If only these shows came with a child-sized warning that stated, "Don't try this at home!" (Yes, this happened to me! My five-year-old thought it was okay to "relieve" himself off the back deck of the house, with his britches around his ankles, after seeing it done on one of the TV programs. My neighbors, who were enjoying an afternoon in their pool with friends, were probably amused, but not impressed. We never watched that show again.)

Inevitably, every child will attempt to challenge the authority of his parents and others and he will likely be disrespectful to boot. The best policy is to have zero tolerance for disrespect. That is the first step toward training our children to respect God. Disrespectful speech and behavior is often born out of anger or frustration when a child doesn't agree with what he is being asked to do. Philippians 2:14 says, "*Do all things without grumbling or questioning"* and that is the behavior we need to train in our little ones. Even though it is really hard to be respectful when he feels life is unfair, he needs to respond with a respectful, "Yes, Mom (or Dad)." Then, hard as it may be, he should follow the Nike plan and simply "Just Do It."

We want our young children to understand and be thankful for the fact that God has placed us, their parents, in a position to watch over and care for them. We love our preschoolers and only want what is best for them. Barbara Curtis, author of *The Mommy Manual*, wrote, "You want (your children's) respect for you to be based not on fear but on a true appreciation of God as their provider, and Mommy and Daddy as the parents God has provided."

And so I pray....

Heavenly Father, You are loving and worthy of respect and praise! Thank you for loving my child and wanting more for him than I can even imagine. I'm sorry that I am not always as consistent as I should be about insisting on respect from my child. I need to remember that you have given me this little one and that automatically makes me worthy of his respect too. Remind me to be a shining example of respecting others for _____ to see. Help me to require respect from him. Show me how to teach _____ that it is normal to feel emotional when he doesn't agree with me, but that he must still respond with respect. Give him a heart that desires to honor and respect his parents on earth and in heaven. Amen.

My Personal Prayer:

How God Answered My Prayer:

Children's Book:

Don't Do That Dexter by Happy Day Books

Parenting Resource:

Don't Make me Count to Three by Ginger Plowman

Chapter Nine
YOU NOT "PANK" ME?
Praying for Your Little One's Honesty

I peered into the faces of each of my three children, hoping to find a clue to the truth. Then my eyes darted back to the kitchen counter. A thick layer of sugar coated everything within a two-foot radius of the sugar bowl. Two telltale Kool-Aid packages lay open on top of the sugar, and where the water had been sloshed over this concoction, red circles were staining my countertop. The mess would wait. I focused on my children's faces again.

Mustering all the self-control I could, I lowered my voice to just above a whisper and insisted, "Please tell Mommy who tried to make Kool-Aid without permission." Looking innocent, three heads began to shake as fingers began to point at their siblings. Obviously, someone was lying to me, and I was crushed that any of my little ones could withhold the truth so effectively. "Okay, you guys, park yourselves right where you are and don't move while I clean up this mess."

With little choice, three kids wisely lined up on the floor in front of the refrigerator. I turned my back to my unidentified culprit and two innocents and went to work sliding sugar off the counter into the trash can. At the same time, I began my monologue… "It makes Mommy and Jesus so sad when one of our children doesn't tell the truth. [It's always good to bring in the "Big Guy" in these situations.] I'm not even angry about the mess here. I'm just so sad that someone isn't telling me the truth." I sensed some squirming behind me on the floor.

Suspecting that the Kool-Aid Caper was instigated by one of my two younger children, I decided that it was best to break from our family policy of immediate and swift consequences for untruths, in order to demonstrate grace while teaching this lesson of honesty. "I don't think I will even punish the person who did this, if they will just tell Mommy the truth."

Then it happened. A little voice behind me asked, "You not pank me?"

Ah-ha, a confession was near. "Nope!" I answered. "If the Kool-Aid maker tells me the truth and helps me clean up this mess, I won't need to punish anyone."

"Ok, then. I did it," confessed Ben.

I have no greater joy than to hear that my children
are walking in the truth.
3 John 1:4

As parents, we cringe when we first catch our preschoolers telling a lie. Sometimes their little eyes or antics give them away. Other times we struggle to determine whether they are indeed lying or telling the truth. This issue is inevitable though, because our children *will* eventually lie. I did it, you did it, and so will they. The important question is whether our children will learn that they can get away with it or not.

Our little ones lie because they mistakenly believe that doing so will somehow help them avoid trouble or embarrassment. Whether our preschooler is stretching the truth, telling a "little white lie," or blurting a boldfaced whopper, we need to address it immediately. If we don't confront our children's lies when they are young, we will be dealing with much worse situations later in their lives.

Our children often learn to tell us lies because we overreact to their mistakes. We want our children to feel safe and comfortable coming to us even when they have really blown it. Also, when we don't tell the truth ourselves, we model poor moral decision-making. The lessons our children learn the best are those they see rather than those they hear.

Children will benefit from learning that the result of honesty is a happy heart, friends and family who trust them, and having handled bad situations the right way. We need our children to understand what God tells us about lying. While honesty may still have a consequence, lying bears an even heavier consequence.

And so I pray...

O Merciful Jesus, Your Word assures me that "Love does not rejoice at wrongdoing, but rejoices with the truth" (1 Corinthians 13:6). I praise you for your Word that guides me on my walk with you and in my parenting. I confess that sometimes I struggle with telling the truth. Forgive me for not always choosing your way and setting a poor example for _____. I pray that he will be filled with your Spirit and that truth will come naturally to him. Show me how to be consistent in my parenting and reveal any dishonesty from _____. Help me not to overreact to lying, and help me know how to discipline and disciple my child regarding the truth. Remind my little one that you are always watching him and that he cannot hide anything from you. May _____ walk in truth with you all the days of his life. Amen.

My Personal Prayer:

How God Answered My Prayer:

Children's Book:

    Piglet Tells the Truth by Mary Manz Simon

Parenting Resource:

    Complete Book of Baby & Child Care: From Pre-Birth through the Teen Years by Dr. Paul Reisser and Dr. James Dobson

Chapter Ten

I'LL PRAY, BUT FIRST...

Praying for Your Little One's Conscience

At the tender age of four, Erica's daughter told her that she accepted Christ. She described to her mom how she was frightened during a thunderstorm, and knew if something happened to her, she didn't have Jesus as her Savior, and wouldn't go to heaven.

Erica couldn't help but feel a little "cheated" that she hadn't been there, hadn't been the one to "lead her to the Lord." She also wondered if Heather had really trusted Christ, being only four and all. Nevertheless, Erica prayed, thanking God for what He'd done in Heather's life, but also asking Him to give her some evidence that the Holy Spirit was living in her little girl, that her salvation was real.

Some time went by, and troubles came into Erica's family. Her sister's husband, a man they all loved very much, was diagnosed with colon cancer at the age of 29.

Erica hung up the phone after hearing one of his surgeries hadn't gone well and the doctors could do no more. In shock and teary at the news, she pulled little Heather to her. "We need to pray, Chicklet. Uncle Joe is very sick, and we need to ask God for some help."

Erica sat down in the glider rocker, and Heather pulled her little wooden chair up to face her mom, as this is how they'd prayed in the past together, face to face, holding hands. Erica bowed her head and was just going to start when Heather pulled her hands away and said, "I can't pray."

Thinking her young daughter must not understand the urgency of the situation, or possibly, she'd caught on to her mother's near panic and despair and was frightened, Erica said, "Oh, Heather, you can always pray. The best time to pray is when you don't know what else to do. God will hear us, and He can make us feel better. Uncle Joe needs our prayers."

"No, Mommy, I can't pray. I have to tell you something first."

Heather went on to confess a minor infraction she'd committed, so minor, if you ask the family today, no one can remember what it was. "I can't talk to Jesus about Uncle Joe until I say I'm sorry for what I did."

Erica was stunned. Here was a glimpse of the "evidence" she'd asked God to show her. Heather's conscience bothered her to the point she knew she couldn't pray and ask God for something when she'd been harboring sin in her heart.

...so that you may be able to discern what is best and
may be pure and blameless until the day of Christ.
Philippians 1:10

"Attention K-Mart shoppers, today in aisle 4 we are having a Blue Light Special on Consciences. Buy one, get one free. This is a great deal for those of you who have more than one child, or need a conscience yourself. Don't walk! Run to aisle 4 now!"

If only it was that easy to assure that your child will develop a healthy conscience. Imagine! Developing an understanding of right and wrong and feeling compelled to do what is right seems to begin in the head and moves to the heart.

When our little ones make choices, it is often based on desire and ease rather than moral right or wrong. Playing with the electrical outlet may seem like a fun past-time and the right choice, that is until Daddy says "no" and moves the little one to a different area of the room. When Jr. returns to the outlet and Daddy says "no" again, this time with a firmer voice, and giving a gentle squeeze to little fingers, Jr. is beginning to understand that playing with outlets is the wrong choice. A few days later when Jr. looks around the room to make sure Daddy isn't around, before crawling over to the outlet, the first indications of conscience are demonstrated. Without parental correction, preschoolers will not develop a healthy conscience.

As our young children get a little older, they can draw on their previous experiences of correction before they make a decision between right and wrong choices. During these years, parents can also be sharing stories with their little ones about what God's Word tells us and how it gives us guidelines for making choices. Now conscience becomes a heart issue as truths are planted in our preschooler's heart and she is able to draw from that knowledge base to determine which choice is best.

Everybody wants to have children who make good choices. Providing consistent, appropriate correction is eternally significant work for parents as we raise children who are drawn to the right choices when faced with the constant temptations of wrong in our world. As parents, we correct our children, but it is the Holy Spirit who will stir their hearts for good. Heather's mother wrote, "The fresh, tender heart of this "baby Christian" showed me what it meant to be sensitive to the Holy Spirit within, showed me what a conscience pricked should lead to in a Christian's life."

And so I pray…

My Jesus, *you are good. Your steadfast love endures forever, and your faithfulness to all generations* (Psalm 100:5). Thank you for your Word and your Truth which shows us how to make right choices. Forgive me for all the times I don't. Jesus, help me remember to be consistent in my parenting and in my correction so _____ will develop a conscience of the heart. Prick the heart of my little one so that he will *"keep a close watch on all he does and thinks. May _____ stay true to what is right so that you, God, will bless him and use him to help others."* (1 Timothy 4:16 NIV 1984). Amen.

My Personal Prayer:

How God Answered My Prayer:

Children's Book:

Right Choices by Kenneth Taylor

Parenting Resource:

Don't Make Me Count to Three by Ginger Plowman

Praying for Your Little One's Development

Chapter Eleven
ENLISTED FOR WAR
Praying for Your Little One's Health

On Thursday, we discovered a dime-sized lump on our preschooler's neck. The following morning the doctor found two additional lumps and testing for lymphoma made the most sense. No parents can prepare themselves for news like this. That evening was spent with my husband and I whispering to each other, crying in the closet, and finding our minds wandering to places we couldn't comprehend. While we waited for the results we imagined our precious, brown-eyed four-year-old with no hair, camped in the hospital, battling this dreaded disease. Even worse, we tried to imagine our life without him, and couldn't.

At four-thirty on Saturday morning, I sat in my prayer chair and tried to feel the arms of Jesus wrapped around me. Instead, I felt that God was telling me to stand up tall and put on His full armor. "Daughter, we are going to war!" I mentally prepared myself to fight on the front lines with my little man as he prepared to battle this potential new enemy.

I rehearsed my battle cry, "We are strong! We are brave! We will win!" My little knowledge of war boils down to movies I have seen and news reports on TV. As a result, the only true battle experience I had was from high school football games. I'm not proud to share that sitting in the stands we would chant at the opposing team, "U...G...L...Y...You ain't got no alibi, you're ugly! Yea! You're ugly!" As I imagined our family standing beside little Ben, fighting the giant enemy, not unlike David did Goliath, I could clearly hear us yelling at the lymphoma, "U…G…L…Y…You ain't got no alibi, you're ugly! Yea! You're ugly!" It was followed by Ben's assuming the stance of a fierce pro-wrestler, arms curled in front of him, tiny muscles bulging as he yelled, "You're going down!"

At noon on Saturday, we learned that the tests were negative. The lumps were still there and would need to be watched and possibly retested, should they change. For now, though, we were being granted a reprieve. Today there will be no war. We are keeping on our armor.

'For I will restore health to you and your wounds I will heal,'
declares the Lord.
Jeremiah 30:17

The health of a preschooler can turn on a dime. Before their afternoon nap they may be perfectly fine; playing, eating, and making a mess. Then they wake up from that afternoon nap with a temperature of 103 and throw up all over your bedroom floor. Call in the troops and the bucket brigade!

It doesn't matter whether it's an unexplained fever, cutting a new tooth, a long run of ear infections, or mysterious lumps that may lead to a terrifying diagnosis. Sometimes the only preparation we have for the battle is to put on the full armor of God and pray for his hand of mercy, strength, and healing. Other times, it is to rest in the everlasting arms of Jesus, accept the diagnosis, and persevere through the difficult circumstances.

Caring for infants, toddlers, and preschoolers is exhausting, but caring for *sick* little ones gives new definition to the term. Who knew it was possible to kneel next to a toddler bed for ten hours with a bucket in hand? Speaking of "in hand".… Have you ever marveled at how God wired parents to instinctively care for sick children? In our house, the same man who, B. C. (Before Children), could sleep through a freight train next door, can now hear his toddler *begin* to gag in the next room at one a.m., hit the floor on a dead run, and catch the up-chuck in his bare hands, before any of it hits the floor! God is good! Nevertheless, too many nights like this, followed by days like this, will wear on a parent. If at all possible, find someone to pitch-hit (or "catch") for you, so that you can get some rest. Carrying for a little one who is physically sick, whiny, and needy is a tremendous amount of work, but it's much worse if you become ill yourself.

When our little ones are sick, we need to reevaluate our priorities and lower our expectations. Chances are we won't get a shower for a day or two, supper will come out of the can or from the delivery man, and the house will undoubtedly be trashed before life returns to normal. Take a deep breathe. Exhale. This too will pass.

Not every childhood illness calls for the cavalry. Sometimes we just have to cling to God as we ride out the storm of a health condition. One of our sons had a recurring skin condition on his leg that was quite unsightly. It didn't really cause him pain or spread to other areas of his body, it just didn't go away and was … well … *gross*. That's how it is with little people. They get funky little things at times, and we just have to deal with it. We can't change it. We can't fix it. We simply have to pray our way through it.

And so I pray…

   Dear Great Physician, My baby is sick. I have not slept and I am physically and emotionally spent. I praise you for being able to restore the health of _____ and heal his wounds if it is your will. Forgive my unbelief when I am weary and feeling sorry for myself. Please place your healing hand on _____ and fill him with strength and comfort. Take away any spirit of fear that my child and I are experiencing. Direct the decisions of his doctors and give us wisdom as his parents. Show us how to best care for _____. Teach me patience and compassion during this time. Help us all rest peacefully in the comfort of your arms. Thank you for *"strengthening us with your power, and according to (your) glorious might, for all great endurance and patience with joy"* (Colossians 1:11). Amen.

My Personal Prayer:

How God Answered My Prayer:

Children's book:

Bear Feels Sick by Karma Wilson

Parenting Resource:

Complete Book of Baby & Child Care: From Pre-Birth through the Teen Years by Dr. Paul Reisser and Dr. James Dobson

Chapter Twelve

DEAR DADDY ...

Praying for Your Little One and Potty Training

When Caleb turned three we took the plunge and committed to tackle potty training. Some time into the process, we found it necessary to e-mail Daddy at work. At the top of the e-mail, we attached a caricature of a little boy standing next to a potty, wearing swim trunks, flippers, water goggles and a snorkel. The e-mail read:

> *Dear Daddy ...*
>
> *This is how you will want to approach the main floor bathroom when you get home. Sorry. I tried to "take care of" my own stinky situation, and Mommy says I used WAY too much toilet paper. Mommy tried to tackle the situation and ended up screaming, chasing "floating things" on the floor, plunging with no success, and mopping like crazy. Now she put a sign on the door that has a potty and an X on it and she said "Don't go IN!" Please hurry home and remember that I love you!*
>
> *Caleb*

Truly, when I agreed to "take the plunge and tackle potty training" I had no idea what those words would really mean.

> *Practice these things, immerse yourself in them,*
> *so that all may see your progress.*
> 1 Timothy 4:15

Ahhh, potty training. We can read all the parenting books, search the internet, pepper our friends with questions and receive unsolicited advice from the generation before us and still the best way to learn the secrets of potty training is to potty train. Everything I know about potty training I learned by teaching my first child to use the potty like a "big girl." Unfortunately, I learned more about what NOT to do than I learned about what worked well. Child number two had it much easier since Mommy was trained in training. So here it is … my three secrets to potty training:

1. Wait. That's it. Wait until your child is physically, emotionally, and mentally ready for the challenge of taking care of business like a big boy or girl. There is no magic age (although "3" worked for us with all three kids). I know families who have had their children trained at 19 months and others at 4 years. None of them sent their children to kindergarten in diapers. This isn't a competition. You will not get a better zip code in heaven if you potty train your child by his second birthday. If you try to train your child before he is ready, you will simply exasperate him and make more work for yourself. Ephesians 6:4 says, *"Fathers [and Mothers], do not provoke your children to anger, but bring them up in the discipline and instruction of the Lord."*

Long before our son officially began potty training, we talked about how great it would be when one day he would get to wear Buzz Lightyear underwear. We watched the older siblings enjoy swimming lessons and said, "Won't it be great when you are using the potty like the big kids and can take swimming lessons too?" (That's the rule at our swimming center, and it has come in handy!) Months before a little bare "bo-hiney" ever sits on our potty mini-seat, we invite him to use the potty. It is usually a casual mention, "Hey, by the way, do you think you might like to sit on the potty before we put on your diaper?" If we are met with a simple, "No," we just fasten that ol' Velcro and away he goes.

2. Don't Despair. When your preschooler has an accident (note that I said "when" and not "if"), don't make a big issue out of it. Getting angry or letting him see or hear your disappointment will only slow down the process. Keep a stash of clean clothes and "undies" somewhere in each bathroom. When the inevitable happens simply say, "Uh oh, that's okay. Let's get you cleaned up and we'll try again." Then remind your little one what he needs to do as soon as he senses the urge to use the bathroom, and send him on his way.

3. Celebrate Big! When your preschooler first starts having success in the bathroom, celebrate! Call everyone in the house to the bathroom and make a tremendous deal out of this occasion! If your child is motivated by gifts, then get yourself some dollar store treasures, special candies, or pennies and nickels ... whatever tickles your big boy or girl's fancy! If your little one is thrilled to earn a sticker on a chart and eventually a diploma as he graduates from diapers, then find yourself a "wall of fame" and let the stickin' begin! As we weaned our children from tangible rewards, we created the "Potty Dance." (That's not the little wiggle they do BEFORE they have to use the potty!) We made up our own little tune to which we would dance around the bathroom, singing "Potty, potty, potty!" It always ended with big hugs and kisses for our big boy or girl as we let them know how thrilled we were with their success and especially with their determination and diligence as they succeeded at potty training.

And so I pray…

Dear Jesus, You are so faithful to hear my prayers and patient in all things. I admit my eagerness to be done with the expense and hassle of diapers sometimes makes me impatient with _____. Please teach me to be kind and patient as my little one grows and matures. Jesus, please help _____ begin to be more aware of her body. Show me the best way to encourage her based on her personality type. I ask that you help me step back and let _____ take ownership of her potty training. May she learn persistence in potty training so she eventually grows to be an adult who is diligent in challenging circumstances. Amen.

My Personal Prayer:

How God Answered My Prayer:

Children's Book:

My Big Boy Undies and *My Big Girl Undies* by Karen Katz

Parenting Resource:

Lifelines: Survival Tips for Parents of Preschoolers by Becky Freeman

Chapter Thirteen
HOUDINI DEMANDS MILK
Praying for Your Little One and Bedtime

Caleb graduated from his crib at sixteen months. It was well before we intended to move him to a "big boy bed," but he gave us no choice. Caleb took his role of the youngest child seriously. He loved to snuggle, nurse, and sleep close to Mommy. We worked very hard to get him to fall asleep in his crib and stay there. Nevertheless, sometime each night he would cry out for me to come and get him. As a sleep deprived mother of three little ones, I would stagger into his bedroom, praying he hadn't woken his brother. I'd carry him back to my bed, let him nurse, and we'd fall back to sleep. Me first. (I'm aware that the baby experts are probably having heart failure about now, and for that I'm sorry, but it worked for this tired mom.)

Some nights I would be so exhausted I wouldn't hear Caleb right away. On one particular night, I heard my little guy calling for me and saying, "Mama, Milk!" I lay very still hoping he might go back to sleep, which did happen occasionally. Soon it was quiet again, and I drifted back to sleep. Not long after I heard a THUMP. I shot out of bed and headed for the hall, certain my three-year-old had fallen out of bed. I was stunned to discover Caleb standing in the hallway with his hands on his hips. "Mama, Milk. Now!"

To this day, I have no idea how that little Houdini escaped from his crib, which had its mattress at the lowest possible setting. I do know it was the last time he ever set foot in that crib. The next day the crib was packed away and the weaning process began.

When you lie down, your sleep will be sweet.
Proverbs 3:24b

If there is a book on getting your child to go to sleep, I've read it and most likely tried it. No kidding. When my friends would bring home their babies from the hospital and they would sleep all night without waking and never look back, I'd secretly pray their next child would wake on the hour, every hour. When the books said my newborn would sleep through the night by the time they were eight weeks old, if only I'd follow their plan, I'd live and breathe that plan. My child did sleep through the night, but not until he was 12 months old. Three children and I didn't get a single sleeper.

My best advice is to find a plan that you, your spouse, and your baby are comfortable with and stick to it. All three of my kids now sleep through the night, most of the time, and with each of them, we used a different approach. If it feels right for you to bring the child to your bed when they wake in the night, fine. If you believe once you shut their bedroom door at night, it will not be opened unless there is an emergency, great. Just remember two things; do what feels right and be in agreement with your spouse.

As infants get a little older, bedtime can still be a huge issue. Preschoolers aren't dummies. They know they are missing out on all the fun when they go to bed. Sleeping … movie … sleeping … movie … there really is no contest here.

Learning to stay in bed alone, soothe themselves, and fall asleep are skills that must be learned, much like potty training. As parents there are several things we can do to help our little ones learn these skills. First, establish a calm bedtime routine and be consistent. If you follow the same routine each night, even very young children will recognize the signal that bedtime is coming. Keep it simple, but don't rush it. Our routine includes a drink, brushing teeth, potty time, a storybook, prayers, and a list of nice things they want to think about as they fall asleep. Whatever you do, keep it the same each night. Leave a list of steps for babysitters, and follow the same schedule when you are away from home, if you can.

Choose a bedtime and keep it the same every night. If your children go to bed at 7:30, then begin the routine fifteen minutes earlier so that they are, in fact, in bed at 7:30. Preschoolers need twelve hours of sleep in a twenty-four hour period. While 7:30 may seem outrageously early to some families, for us it worked. We value our time together as a couple and need that time to connect. In some homes, Mom or Dad may not get home until later and early bedtimes rob the family of together time. The important thing is to find a bedtime that works for your family and be consistent.

Finally, don't reward your child for getting out of bed. When our little ones get out of bed and are given another drink, time to rock or snuggle, or one more story, they learn that sneaking out of bed is acceptable. When preschoolers have gone through their bedtime routine, they need to learn that the routine won't be extended or repeated. Instead, celebrate their "staying in bed" behaviors! Reward them with stickers in the morning when they stay in bed all night and lots of hugs and kisses for a job well done.

Learning to get to sleep and stay asleep in one's own bed demonstrates self-control and perseverance.

And so I pray…

Thank you, God, for restful nights. I praise you for being a sanctuary for a tired parent. Thank you for inviting, "Come to me, all who labor and are heavy laden … and I will give you rest" (Matthew 11:28). I'm there! Please be with all of us as _____ learns the skills necessary to fall asleep on his own and stay in his bed all night. Show us which plan will work best for our family. Help me be consistent with the routine and the plan we chose to follow. May _____ rest peacefully tonight and be ready to enjoy the new day you will give us tomorrow. Amen

My Personal Prayer:

How God Answered My Prayer:

Children's Book:

Bed Time Blessings (Little Blessings) by Dandi Daley Mackall

Parenting Resource:

Lifelines: Survival Tips for Parents of Preschoolers by Becky Freeman

Chapter Fourteen

NO REGRETS?

Praying for Your Little One and Picking up Toys

One evening, a couple of weeks before Christmas, four-year-old Timothy was getting ready for bed. At the same time, his mother realized he had not yet picked up his toys in the living room. Timothy knew the family rule was if toys weren't picked up before bedtime, in the morning he would find them boxed up and in the "Uh Oh! Toy Time Out" box. The return date of the treasure was determined by the parent who packed them away or a chore could be completed in exchange for the toy. Due to his natural laid-back tendency, Timothy asked, "Mom, if I don't put away my toys, how many days will it be before I can play with them again?"

Mom explained, "Buddy, if you don't put your toys away now, they will be in Time Out for three days. That means you will go to sleep three nights and wake up three mornings before you will get to play with them again. If you don't clean up your toys now, you might really regret it later."

Timothy spent a few more minutes pondering this new information. Then he announced, "I can handle that!" and off he went to bed, believing he had won the better end of the deal.

The next morning Timothy and his brother, Thomas, woke up and tore open a small gift as part of their advent calendar. Timothy received a toy that he had been anxious to receive. In his excitement, he grabbed his new toy and ran to the living room to add it to the rest of the set.

There he stopped, for it was then he realized his toys were gone … for three days. He knew now he had made a terrible choice the night before.

> *Whatever you do, work heartily,*
> *for the Lord and not for men,*
> *knowing that from the Lord you will receive*
> *the inheritance as your reward.*
> Colossians 3:23-24

Cleaning up toys is not as much fun as playing with them. I can relate. Putting away laundry is not as much fun as wearing clothes, and stocking the fridge and pantry with groceries isn't as much fun as eating. It still has to be done though. We model the importance of cleaning up toys when we do actually put away the clean laundry and groceries. When our children see piles around the house, without intending to we give them the message that messes are all right.

With young children, we can help them learn to clean up their toys when we have a special place for toys to be stored. Living by the mantra, "a place for everything and everything in its place" will result in a neat and orderly home. After you have established a place for toys to live, then teach your children that when they are finished with one toy, they should put it in its home before they play with another toy.

On those occasions when their play area or living room has been taken over by the toys and the room is a disaster, it will be necessary to help your child break this overwhelming job into smaller tasks. First, put all the baby dolls to bed and then tackle the puzzle pieces.

It is helpful to predetermine several times throughout the day when Mom or Dad will call for a Ten-Minute Tidy. During these events, a timer is set for ten minutes and the entire family pitches in to straighten up the house and tidy the toys. Cleaning up can be fun when the family works as a team and they all sing loudly while doing it.

When toys aren't picked up and put back in their homes, then they are homeless and they have to live in a box on the shelf for a few days. Setting the box where it can be seen but not reached adds greater impact to the consequence of a Toy Time Out. Sometimes toys need to be bagged up and put away for an even longer period of time. These toys are welcomed back with enthusiasm and appreciated on a rainy day.

Teaching our preschoolers to be responsible for the toys they have is important. As they learn to clean up their toys, they demonstrate appreciation for the blessings God has given them. They also benefit from experiencing the satisfaction of working hard and with a sweet spirit.

And so I pray…

My Holy God, You are faithful in all you say and do. Thank you for helping me clean up the messes in my life. Forgive me for the piles of emotional and physical "stuff" I have ignored. Help me set a good example for _____ as he learns to work hard and with a right attitude. Please help me be consistent with _____ as I train him to clean up his toys. I know toys are just a piece of the bigger puzzle. I pray that by learning to clean up his toys, _____ also learns the joy of working hard and with a cheerful heart, so one day he can use these skills in his work for you. Amen.

My Personal Prayer:

How God Answered My Prayer:

Children's Book:

Let's Be Helpful by P.K. Hallinan

Parenting Resource:

The Parenting Survival Guide by Dr. Todd Cartmell

Chapter Fifteen

SLOPPY JOE

Praying for Your Little One's Speech and Language

As my husband and I rocked each of our three children as babies, we looked into their little faces and wondered what it would be like when they learned to talk. How might their voices sound? Would their first word be "Mama" or "Dada"? We hung on their early coos and babbles and engaged in mock conversations with our infants.

Eventually our little ones caught on to the joys of language and began stringing words together. Sometimes the things they said made us smile as they experimented with their newfound speech skills. Car rides seemed to provide the most entertaining material from our children.

Several years later, I was driving with my three-year-old son, who was playing with a G.I. Joe action figure. Once again, the minivan provided the stage for an entertaining commentary. As he practiced his best "tough guy" voice, we heard him command, "You go get 'em, Sloppy Joe!"

With the dawning of their speech abilities our children also began trying out words for their shock value. Sometime before his second birthday, our youngest son discovered that when he muttered "baby poopy" under his breath, he was rewarded with gales of laughter from his older siblings. This only encouraged his naughtiness and before long, the seemingly harmless phrase was used often and with great gusto. No longer did the listener need to bend an ear to hear him. He used his phrase whenever he was feeling silly, bored, ignored, or angry. It became his mantra when he didn't want his diaper changed, when his brother didn't share a toy, or when he thought he could get a laugh from some unsuspecting bystander.

Let no corrupting talk come out of your mouths,
but only such as is good for building up, as fits the occasion,
that it may give grace to those who hear.
Ephesians 4:29 (ESV)

It seems as though we spend the first twelve months of our child's life teaching him to talk and the next twelve years teaching him to control his tongue. As parents, it's sometimes hard to know when our little ones are "just being preschoolers" and when they are intentionally being naughty and have pushed the limits of their speech exploration too far.

Speech is a precarious issue. We want to celebrate our children's successes and encourage their efforts. We even want to rejoice over the errors they make. How fabulous that our children aren't afraid to "try on" words that they have heard, and risk botching their usage, without missing a beat. We are delighted when our toddlers grasp the meaning of a "big" word and use it exhaustively. Our daughter loved to say "actually" when she was three. She tacked it on to nearly every sentence she said, making her sound nearly as precocious as we knew her to be.

When our children use words that are less than wholesome or try to shock us with a perceived naughty word, we can't help but feel disappointment and perhaps a sense of failure. It seems that these words are not always saved for the privacy of our homes either. Oh, no, it is even more fun for our little ones to try on their new words at the grocery store checkout and, even worse, at church or for their grandparent. We cringe and wish we could sink into the floor. Quickly we must pull ourselves up off the linoleum, however, and correct the offensive tongue. In many cases, our little ones have no idea what they have just said, so the first infraction can be addressed by telling the child that "this" word is naughty and shouldn't be used. Future uses of the word will need to be followed up with an appropriate consequence.

In our home, we refer to inappropriate language as "potty words." The kids came up with this term themselves after we explained that using naughty words is like drinking water from the toilet; it leaves a terrible taste in your mouth and makes you sick to your stomach. We stressed that drinking potty water is NEVER done; just like saying "potty words" is also never to be done and will result in big trouble (like cleaning potties)!

So we talk to them about nice words that are clean and soothing to other's ears. We also talk about words that aren't nice and are unpleasant to hear. Sometimes we simply ignore their unwholesome talk, not giving attention to that which doesn't bring God glory, and other times we have to dole out some cleaning chores.

And so I pray…

My Faithful God, How wonderful and creative you are for giving us such rich language. I delight in your good gifts! I confess that I don't always set the best example for my child. Sometimes my own speech is out of control and I use language that is displeasing to you. God, forgive me. Help me demonstrate for _____ the kind of language that glorifies you. Please help _____ have appropriate speech and language development. Remind me to celebrate his successes and show him my pleasure with his new skills. Make _____'s word choices wholesome and pleasing, so that one day he can be an effective witness to the unblemished truth of the gospel. Amen.

My Personal Prayer:

How God Answered My Prayer:

Children's Book:

> *God, I Need to Talk to you about Bad Words* by Susan K. Leigh

Parenting Resource:

> *See How They Run* by Lorilee Cracker

Chapter Sixteen
FACE OF PAIN
Praying for Your Little One's Safety

We have a very strict policy that there is to be absolutely no jumping on the bed. (Except in hotels, but that's another story.) It soon became clear that we had never mentioned there was also to be no jumping "off" the bed. As a direct result of this omission, donning his dishtowel Superman cape, our four-year-old son "flew" off his bed. His foot pushed against the mattress as he launched himself into the air, causing his mattress to slide away from the metal bed frame. The protruding frame caught our superhero's side and kept a chunk of flesh as a souvenir. The resulting gap in his side meant a four-hour visit to the emergency room and three new stitches.

I knelt beside the examining table while my little guy was being stitched. Petrified, he flew into helpless hysterics. I held his upper body and face, resting his forehead against my own. The look in his eyes broke my heart. He'd sob and scream, "Somebody's hurting me. Don't let him do it, Mommy!" In truth, he was numb and couldn't feel a thing, but his fear was real, and I felt helpless. When the final stitch was completed he rolled on his back and between hiccupped sobs, offered the doctor a weak, "Fank you."

Blessed is the one who considers the poor!
In the day of trouble the LORD delivers him;
the LORD protects him and keeps him alive;

he is called blessed in the land;
you do not give him up to the will of his enemies.
The LORD sustains him on his sickbed;
in his illness you restore him to full health.
Psalm 41:1-3 (ESV)

Tumbling down a flight of stairs, falling out of bed, swallowing a penny, sticking a soybean up the nose, or running into the street … these are some of a parent's worst fears. As preschoolers become more independent, they flex their muscles and explore their world. Every step further away from our side invites new and unforeseen dangers. We childproof our homes; buy and install electric outlet protectors, latches on cupboards, and doorknob covers. We caution our children about things that cause "owies," which shouldn't be touched. We teach our children about strangers and hope they take to heart our cautions without being fearful of all new people. Despite our best efforts, however, they still get hurt.

It is difficult to watch our children when they are in pain, even if it's for their own good, as in the case of immunizations or stitches. We hold their faces close, look into their eyes and reassure them, "Here I am. I love you. I'm not leaving. I know it hurts and I know you are scared. You will be okay." As we demonstrate the truth of our love for our preschoolers, they catch a glimpse of their Heavenly Father's love too. How often he holds our faces in his hands! He assures us of his presence, love, comfort, and hope. Oh, how it must grieve him to see and feel our pain, even when it's for our own good. While we pray for the safety of our children and we make efforts to protect them from danger, we must also teach them to be thankful that in their pain they are never alone.

And so I pray...

My Precious God in Heaven, How awesome it is to sing your praise! You are my protector and my stronghold! Your name is a strong tower and you invite me to run to you. Thank you! I admit, sometimes as a parent of young children, I try to be SuperParent and attempt to be all things to my children, including their protector. Every day I am learning I can't always do this. I can't possibly be everywhere my child goes and ensure a safe environment. Father, you know the situations _____ will encounter today. If it is your will, please keep him from harm. Help him make choices that won't put him in danger. When _____ is hurt, hold his face in your comforting hands, and remind him you will never leave him, nor forsake him (Joshua 1:5). May my child "dwell in safety" for you "surround him all day long" (Deuteronomy 33:12). Help me, God, to remember you love my children even more than I do. Thanks be to you, our comforter and protector. Amen.

My Personal Prayer:

How God Answered My Prayer:

Children's Book:

> *Percy Plays it safe* by Stuart J. Murphy

Parenting Resource:

> *Complete Book of Baby & Child Care: From Pre-Birth through the Teen Years* by Dr. Paul Reisser and Dr. James Dobson

Chapter Seventeen

Rx: PAJAMA DAY

Praying for Your Little One and Morning Routines

On yet another early morning, I mustered up as much enthusiasm as I could and sang, "Good Morning to you, Good Morning to you!" But even my boisterous singing and silly dancing couldn't inspire my sleepy little ones as I coaxed them out of their snug cocoons to face another busy day.

"I don't want to go to preschool … daycare … church … the grocery store …" they whined. I'd heard it nearly every morning for weeks and to be honest, I couldn't have agreed more. We all needed a break, but responsibilities and obligations weighed on me, and I promised soon we would take a day off.

Then as I guided my daughter to the bathroom, with a hand on her back, forcing her cement-like feet to move, I heard her weary voice whimper, "I just want to stay in my pajamas." I sighed and then realized that, so did I.

"We will!" I announced.

"What?" Kadi asked, looking confused.

"We will stay in our pajamas today! All day!"

Kadi looked at me as if I had lost my mind. Had she heard "Miss-Mommy-Hit-the-floor-running-and-don't-come-to-breakfast-until-you-are-dressed" right?

Indeed she had. That was the first official Pajama Day at the Tiede house. We didn't get dressed all day. We played, read books, watched movies, napped, and ate all three meals in our pajamas. Pajama Day was the perfect prescription for the Get-Up-and-Go Blues.

This is the day that the Lord has made; let us rejoice and be glad in it.
Psalm 118:24

Some children are just not morning people. It's a fact. We can engage in the Every Morning War or we can deal with it. If you know you have to get up and go in the morning and you have a little one who needs extra time in the morning, then by all means, allow that extra time. Wake your preschooler earlier so he has more time to wake up and go through the morning routine without having to rush.

Make sure you stick to a consistent routine and if there is time, allow for a reward after the routine is accomplished. For example, once your young child has dressed, completed their bathroom jobs, and eaten breakfast, allow for a few minutes of cartoons, time to play with a special toy, or read a book before you head out the door.

The absolute best way to assure a stress-free morning is to establish a great bedtime routine. If you must leave the house early in the morning, then you may need your child to have an earlier bedtime. When children have adequate sleep, they can deal with mornings better. Include morning preparations as part of your bedtime routine. Line up diaper bags, backpacks, purses, and shoes at the door before everyone goes to bed. Lay out clothes for everyone before bed too. The few minutes it takes to do this in the evening will save you from a mad scramble in the morning.

For some families, a parent's job demands that children get up early and leave the house with their parents. However, sometimes children have to get up and go early, simply for the sake of keeping an unnecessarily busy, parent-driven schedule. Ouch. If those words pricked your conscience, then clear your plate that is too full of busyness and stay home a couple of days a week. Children need the predictability and stability of just being home. The preschool years fly by so quickly. What a shame if children never enjoy these years in the haven they call home.

Each morning God gives us twenty-four hours to use for His glory. If we start off the morning on the wrong foot with our preschoolers, we set the tone for the rest of the day. On the other hand, if we are pro-active and meet each morning with the hope of something wonderful God has planned for us and for our children, then we are sure to enjoy each day's blessings.

And so I pray…

Gracious God, Thank you for each new day you give me! Show me how you want me to use this day for your glory. I pray you will help me be organized and diligent in my preparations for each morning so my family can enjoy all you have in store for us today. Please help _____ get wonderful rest at night so he can wake up refreshed and ready to go. Remind me to be patient with him on his slow mornings and to use encouraging, not critical, words. May you walk with _____ this morning and the rest of his days. Amen.

My Personal Prayer:

How God Answered My Prayer:

Children's Book:

Sophie and Sam: When to Say "Yes" and When to Say "No" by Tori Cloud

*This book also has stories covering; honesty, sharing, whining, respect, clean-up, meanies, following rules, manners, and arguing. Highly Recommended!

Parenting Resource:

First-Time Mom by Dr. Kevin Leman

Praying for Your Little One's Social Skills

Chapter Eighteen
CHEETOS® RECOVERY TEAM
Praying for Your Little One's Manners

As my four-year-old rounded the table with a mounding handful of Cheetos piled in his hands, one tragically escaped his fingers and tumbled to the floor. In the voice of a true rescue hero, Ben cried out, "Daddy, quick! Grab that Cheeto before Shasta eats it!" Shasta, the twelve-year-old family Pomeranian routinely patrols the area under the kitchen table for any such accidents that might benefit her taste buds.

Daddy, always fast on his toes, ran to the Cheeto and grabbed it up, saving it from the clutches of sure destruction. Gloating about his achievement he announced to the crowd of three, around the table, "I was proud to be a member of this recovery team."

I shook my head and smiled. Boys. Feeling the need to do the "mom thing" and take advantage of a teachable moment, I asked Ben, "What do you need to tell Daddy for recovering your Cheeto?"

Looking his daddy straight in the eye, Ben announced, "Good catch, Daddy!"

May you always be doing those good,
kind things which show that you are a child of God,
for this will bring much praise and glory to the Lord.
Philippians 1:11 (TLB)

Teaching our children to use "thank you," "please," "I'm sorry" and countless other social graces when they are necessary, is a constant challenge for parents of preschoolers. In our home, we made a practice of teaching each of our children to use baby sign language long before they were able to effectively use their speech to communicate. Sign language allowed us to get on with the important business of communicating with our little ones and teaching them manners. "Thank you" and "please" were among the first five signs our toddlers learned. Because their early communication was limited to words associated with manners, those words seem to have stuck.

Whether or not your child learns sign language, teaching even your youngest children to say "please" and "thank you" is advantageous. A simple "peeeeeeee" (loosely interpreted as "please") can help your little one get many of her needs met; more Cheerios, a drink of juice, or five more minutes in her bubble bath. Teach these words early, insist on them even, and they will become a life-long habit.

How often are we disappointed or frustrated when our children respond inappropriately or worse, not at all, when a respectful show of manners was needed? When this happens and you are alone with your child, it is very important to correct their manners right away. Make it a game and try again! When your little Neanderthal throws his coat on the floor and demands, "Give me juice," instead of blowing a gasket, you might say, "Hey Big Guy, let's try that again with a 'please'." You might have to repeat this a few times until Mr. Bossy Head decides to say "please" nicely, at which time you can make a grand affair of getting him some juice. (Then tell him to pick up his coat … please!)

Don't you just want to melt into the floor when your preschooler doesn't use his manners with people outside of your home? If your child has forgotten to use his manners, the sign language can come in handy here. Suppose your child was given a gift or a compliment and she has forgotten to say "thank you." You can discretely sign "thanks" when your child looks at you, which will serve as her cue to say the words herself. This eliminates the need for us to use that good old parent phrase, "What do you say?" If your child is just refusing to use pleasant manners, you can explain, "We are still working on this" and then remove her from the situation. Of course, don't forget to really "work on this" as soon as you have your child alone.

I believe that God also feels disappointed and frustrated when we don't respond to Him as we should. When God faithfully answers our prayers, actively moves in our lives, or blesses our boots off, we sometimes respond with, "This is just what I wanted! Great!" or worse yet, we are silent. Instead, we need to be thanking our Father who meets all of our needs and provides blessings beyond measure. If our children do not learn to exercise the appropriate use of manners with people around them, then giving thanks, asking politely, or taking responsibility and apologizing will never be internalized or come naturally. When children don't gain this skill, they aren't equipped to apply it when they communicate with their heavenly Father either.

And so I pray....

Heavenly Father, I rejoice in knowing that as your offspring, I have the amazing privilege of your perfect teaching. You are always a gentleman, never rude or demanding. Your gentle spirit and gracious ways are familiar to me. This is the way you desire your children to relate to you. I pray that _____ would have a tender heart that is thankful, remorseful, and well-mannered. Please help me model that behavior in my own interactions with _____ and with others, that my child may see me as a worthy example. Help me be gentle, kind, and patient in my direction and guidance of _____. Make clear to me the teachable moments. I purposely place myself in the path of your counsel. May _____ have manners that are pleasing to you and which glorify your name. Amen.

My Personal Prayer:

How God Answered My Prayer:

Children's Book:

Panda is Polite by Dr. Mary Manz Simon

Parenting Resource:

Don't Make Me Count to Three by Ginger Plowman

Chapter Nineteen
RAW OR COOKED?
Praying for Your Little One and Mealtimes

In general, Dawn and George's family enjoys a fairly healthy diet, but getting enough vegetables tends to be a bit of a challenge. With four-year-old Elijah, they have learned not to force the issue. In time, he will be in the mood for vegetables and eat enough to last him for the week. He has been known to eat almost twenty baby carrots in one sitting, that is, as long as they are not crunchy. He has not yet developed an appreciation for raw vegetables.

For Elijah's family, cake is a rare treat. However, for birthdays they sometimes partake of three different cakes at three different parties – one with Dawn's relatives, one with my George's relatives, and one with friends. For his fourth birthday Elijah's parents let him choose his cake from the bakery, and it turned out to be a carrot cake. One of his three parties was at a park with two long slides, a sand pit with diggers, and other miscellaneous playground equipment. Elijah and his cousins were too busy playing to be interested in coming back to the picnic table to eat, even for birthday cake.

A couple of days later Elijah asked for a piece of his cake. George took the cake out of the refrigerator and got ready to cut a slice for Elijah. There wasn't a whole lot left of the cake by this time, but a few of the frosting carrots, which decorated the top, remained. Not surprisingly Elijah asked for a piece with a carrot on it. The more frosting the better, right? Then he thought a minute and asked, "Is the carrot raw or cooked?"

So whether you eat or drink or whatever you do,
do it all for the glory of God.
1 Corinthians 10:31

In more families with preschoolers than not, the call to dinner could just as easily be a call to "man your stations!" Dinnertime has the potential of being an all-out war. Part of the problem is that by the time General Mom comes to the table, she has already spent considerable time preparing for this battle. Food has been cooked, baby food warmed, bibs donned, booster seats and high chairs buckled, meat cut, and sippy cups poured. Have you ever wondered why Mom doesn't immediately open her eyes after grace? Once she rouses herself, she is met with a chorus of, "What is THIS?" and "Yucky! I don't like it!" *Sigh*. Most families need a battle plan. Here it is.

Rules of Mealtime Combat: (Okay, so I'm taking this battle theme a little too far. Sorry.)

1) Mealtime is at the table. Serve and eat food at the kitchen or dining room table, not in the family room on the couch or on the floor (except in special circumstances).

2) No TV. Television during mealtime serves as an uncontrollable magnet. As parents, we must become verbally repetitive, threatening to "turn off that TV if you don't start to eat now!" Yeah, right. They know you don't mean it either.

3)   Stay in your chair. When little ones are strapped into a high chair or booster seat, this isn't a real issue, but once they break free from this slight form of bondage, they can go crazy. Make a rule that everyone stays in their seat unless they have permission to leave the table. If they get off their chair once, they get a warning. If they leave the table again, they lose their plate and dinner is done for them.

4)   One "No, thank you" bite. Young children have very sensitive taste buds and can be turned off by certain textures. This is normal. If your children only eat one or two favorite foods for a few weeks, they aren't going to shrivel up. As long as they are healthy and not losing weight, they will be all right. Nevertheless, if you only feed them fish sticks or chicken nuggets they will never learn to eat other things. Instead, give your child one, child-sized bite of foods that are new or are not their favorites. Nothing on the table should be exempt unless there are allergies. Then tell your child that they are expected to eat that one bite. If they are offered more, they may choose to either accept more or simply say, "No, thank you." If you implement the "no, thank you" bite rule, then your children will be encouraged to at least sample new foods and eventually will learn to like the variety.

5)   Serve smaller portions. Little children have little stomachs. Serve them small portions and when that is gone, they can eat more and feel successful.

6)   Close the café. You can hang up your short order cook apron. If you fix different foods for everyone at the table, it is not only terribly expensive but exhausting, and your children's belief that the world revolves around them is confirmed. Make sure you serve at least one thing at each meal your child will like. If all your child eats is one bite of casserole, one bite of vegetable and a plate of apple slices, they will

be just fine.

7) <u>Solids first.</u> If your little ones are filling up on juice, milk, or water they aren't going to have room for their meal. Make sure they eat some of their meal before you even serve liquids. This will eliminate the problem of full tummies before they even begin their dinner. Our daughter used to drink a quart of apple juice every day, and I wondered why she didn't want to eat! Yes, I learned rule 7 the hard way.

8) <u>Smaller snacks.</u> Snacks sabotage meals. Period. If you must serve snacks, keep them healthy and small.

9) <u>Pokey Joe.</u> If you have a Pokey Joe or a grazer, set the timer. It shouldn't take more than thirty minutes for even a slow eater to finish a meal. Tell your little guy that when the timer rings, the table will be cleared. Believe me, your preschooler is going to test you on this one and may go to bed hungry at least one time. Most pediatricians will tell you, however, that you will not do your little one irreparable harm if he or she goes to bed hungry once.

That's it. Nine rules for mealtime combat. Once your family learns and applies these, call an armistice and sign the treaty. Congratulations! Your family can enjoy peaceful meals together and spend time enjoying fellowship and celebrating the blessings of fun, food, and family.

And so I pray…

Faithful God, we praise you for being our Provider. You give us food, strength, and health. Thank you. Please put a hedge of protection and blessing around _____ and everything he has (Job 1:10). Help him be a good eater at mealtimes. Show me, as _____'s parent, how to be consistent with mealtime rules and routines so meals can be a time of peaceful fellowship and not frustration. I pray that _____ gives you the glory in whatever he eats or drinks (1 Corinthians 10:31) and that he nourishes his soul through the reading of your Word (Matthew 4:4). Amen.

My Personal Prayer:

How God Answered My Prayer:

Children's Book:

I Don't Like It by Heather Gemmen

Parenting Resource:

Lifelines: Survival Tips for Parents of Preschoolers by Freeman

Chapter Twenty
THANK YOU, GOD
Praying for Your Little One and Sharing

Our family loves to spend time with friends. It is not uncommon on a Saturday night for us to invite another family over for dinner. The kids play and the adults visit. It's comfortable. We have graduated from needing booster seats for our own children, but when friends with younger children visit, we pull out the booster seat and strap it to a chair. If a bib or sippy cup is needed, we pull one out without a second thought.

One evening we were enjoying time with friends who brought along 18-month-old Jacob. Jacob is a little tank, and as cute as he is solid. Jacob toddled around after our three- and five-year-old sons, which they thought was great. Three-year-old Caleb willingly brought Jacob toys and books. Before our friends left for the evening we offered to let them borrow a pair of Caleb's pajamas, as Jacob would likely fall asleep on the way home. This rock solid little guy wore the same size as our youngest child and we were thrilled that this plan was going to work out so well. As we pulled Caleb's fireman jammies over Jacob's head, my little guy's expression caught my eye. He looked none too thrilled, but didn't say a word.

After waving good-bye to our friends, we marched our three sleepy heads up the stairs and into their bedrooms. I knelt by Caleb's bed, ready to hear his precious, preschool "thank you, God" prayers. This time they sounded more than a little bit forced and slightly irritated. "Thank you, God, that I gave Jakey my toys. Thank you, God, that I gave *Jakey* my sippy cup. Thank you, God that I gave JAKEY … (long pause) … my fireman jammies. He will give it back? Amen."

I had never considered the sacrifice my three-year-old was making that night; sharing all of his treasured belongings with his friend. While it pained him to watch his jammies walk out the door on another little boy's back, he never fussed. Then I got on my knees again, "Heavenly Father, thank you for this precious child. May this generous boy, himself be blessed (Proverbs 22:9). Amen."

And do not forget to do good and to share with others,
for with such sacrifices God is pleased.
Hebrews 13:16

Have you ever purchased a brand new car with less than 20 miles on the odometer and driven it off the lot and into your own garage? And if a neighbor had the nerve to ask you if he could borrow it that afternoon for a quick trip out of town, how did you feel? Okay, so it's not very likely this has really happened, but is it so very different than asking a four-year-old birthday girl to share her brand new, just opened, baby doll with her cousin during the party? Sharing is hard.

As we teach our preschoolers to share, they need to understand they are not being asked to share everything with everybody, all the time. Some things are treasured items that do not need to be shared. When guests are around, however, those possessions should be put away.

Children can also learn they have some choices when they are asked to share. They can say they are using the toy, but their friend or sibling can use it soon. Sometimes they may choose to share the toy if they are not using it or are finished with it. They can also suggest that they play with the toy together. No matter how they choose to share the toy, they need to be respectful and kind to the person who is asking for the prized item. People are much more important than things. If your little one throws a temper tantrum when they have to share, then they may need some time away from those who are playing nicely.

Timers work well in our home when everyone "needs" to play with the same toy. It's hard to argue with a beeping box when it's time to pass the toy to the next person.

When you do catch your toddler generously sharing a toy, celebrate! Let him know you are so proud of him. If it's appropriate, find something special he can enjoy now as a surprise bonus for sharing his belonging.

Have I said sharing is hard? Generosity just doesn't come as naturally as selfishness. The number one way we can help our children overcome self-centeredness and greed is to model sacrificial giving ourselves. Our preschoolers need to see us sharing the good gifts God has given us with those in need. It can be as simple as a cup of sugar for the neighbor, or as extreme as sharing your home with a family in need. Our children are like little, walking spyglasses, always watching and learning from our example. There is a beautiful song that says, "May the footprints that we leave, lead them to believe. May all who come behind us find us faithful." As our little ones follow our footsteps, may they know we believe "it is more blessed to give than to receive" (Acts 20:35).

And so I pray…

Gracious God, You are the giver of all good things. Thank you for everything you have shared with me and given to my family. Please forgive me for all the times that I have been selfish and greedy with the blessings you have given me. Help me "shine as lights in the world," sharing your Word and your gifts with others (Philippians 2:15). Make me a worthy example to _____. May he develop a generous spirit. Show _____ how to become a cheerful giver (2 Corinthians 9:7). May he treat others with the same love you have shown to him. Amen.

My Personal Prayer:

How God Answered My Prayer:

Children's Book:

Lion Can Share by Dr. Mary Manz Simon

Parenting Resource:

Don't Make Me Count to Three by Ginger Plowman

Chapter Twenty-One
CAN SHE FIX IT?
Praying for Your Little One and Tattling

Kaitlin and Kalli were playing together in their room while their mom worked on supper in the kitchen. Soon Mom heard the familiar sounds of a disagreement, but she decided to wait and see if the girls could sort it out themselves rather than getting involved in yet another sister-tiff.

Pretty soon it got quiet and Kaitlin appeared in the kitchen. "Mommy," she tattled, "Kalli had a bad attitude, but I fixed it."

Oh, my! The girls' mother couldn't imagine how her three-and-a-half-year-old could have "fixed" the attitude of her two-year-old sister. And leave it to an older child to tattle on the baby and make herself look good at the same time. Kaitlin would need a little lesson in the fact that we can't fix other people's bad attitudes, only Jesus can. "Oh, really!" she replied. "Just how, exactly, did YOU fix Kalli's attitude?"

Kaitlin explained, "Kalli didn't want to play my way, and I told her she shouldn't be mad. I said she needed to pray that Jesus would give her a better attitude."

Oh, what the girls' mother would have given to see Kaitlin leading her little sister in prayer for a better attitude. Apparently, she already understood the lesson about Jesus.

Then Kalli joined her mother and sister in the kitchen. She looked up at her mom with big eyes and said, "I sorry." She got the lesson too.

So then let us pursue what makes for peace
and for mutual upbuilding.
Romans 14:19 (ESV)

"Mom, Caleb tried to bite me!" "Ben frewed my ball outside!"
"He started it!" "I did not!" Aaaagggghhhh! Tattling. It's almost as
painful to listen to as fingernails dragging across a blackboard. (Do
they even make blackboards anymore?)

Listening to tattling turns every parent into Judge Mommy or
Daddy. If you listen, you will have to find someone guilty or declare a
mistrial. As parents of preschoolers, we have to be discerning about
what is worth hearing and what can be ignored. We also have to teach
our children what should be reported and what they need to work out
on their own.

Most of the time, the primary objective of a tattler is to get the
other poor soul in big trouble. Preschoolers don't just squeal on their
siblings, they even squeal on their friends. First-borns are ruthless
about narking on their pals. When a little one comes to us for the sole
purpose of getting their playmate in trouble, we can respond with a
simple, "thank you" and send them on their way. If we don't give any
additional response and we don't get involved, our preschooler will
soon figure out we aren't going to do anything to help their cause and
they might as well not bother tattling. If our preschooler, however,
comes to report a genuine woe, we can get involved and provide
appropriate correction. In the end, little ones discover that their parents
will only rally if the truth is being told and tattling will decrease.

Tattlers are often sharing a biased, partial account of what really happened. We want our preschoolers to understand that only Jesus can judge others, and we must each take responsibility for our own behavior. Learning this truth as a child will free them of great disappointment with imperfect people in an imperfect world, as they grow up.

And so I pray...

Merciful God, thank you for being just and loving to your children. Forgive me for the times that I am critical of others and am quick to judge. Help me demonstrate tolerance, cooperation, forgiveness, and truth to my preschooler. Grant _____ a quiet tongue when it comes to tattling. Help him recognize when he needs to come to me with a true and genuine issue that requires my involvement. Show _____ how to be a peacemaker among his playmates. May _____ speak truth in love so he can show his friends and siblings how to walk in your ways. Amen.

My Personal Prayer:

How God Answered My Prayer:

Children's Book:

    The Tattletale by Lynn Downey

Parenting Resource:

    Creative Correction: Extraordinary Ideas for Everyday Discipline
by Lisa Welchel

Chapter Twenty-Two
ISAAC'S YOUR BUDDY
Praying for Your Little One and Their Friendships

Glory turned off the radio in her van and eavesdropped with delight on the backseat debate between her three-year-old daughter and two-year-old son about their friends.

"I love to play with Elaine. Elaine is my friend. She's my best friend," Ann announced to her brother.

"Elaine is my friend," parroted Peter.

"No, Elaine is not your friend. She's MY friend!"

"Elaine is my friend."

"No, Elaine is NOT your friend."

"Elaine is my friend."

"Elaine is MY friend. You play with Isaac. I play with Elaine. She's a girl and she's my friend. Isaac is a boy, so he's your buddy," Ann clarified.

"Elaine is a boy. Isaac's my buddy," Peter tried, quite pleased with his new understanding.

Tense and exasperated Ann spat, *"No! Elaine is a GIRL! Isaac is a boy. You're a boy too, so Isaac is your BUDDY! Elaine is MY friend because she is a GIRL!"*

Peter smiled from ear to ear, confident he got it now. "Elaine is my friend. Isaac's your buddy," he proclaimed with a confident nod.

"MOM!"

A friend loves at all times.
Proverbs 17:17

Before the age of five, children have very little say about whom they want for friends. The children of your friends become their friends. We took our five-week-old son to the hospital with us when our friends gave birth to their own son. I clearly remember sticking my son up to the new baby and cooing, "Ben, meet your new buddy, Drew." These two really did take to each other and share a brother-like bond today, but they certainly didn't have much choice in the beginning.

Knowing their friends will influence our preschoolers, for the good and the bad, should put parents on the alert. We need to exercise wisdom as we choose playmates for our little ones. How do they talk to their parents and treat their siblings? Do they use appropriate language? Are they kind to others? Do they share similar life experiences? We need to be cautious as we choose friends for our little ones because they are vulnerable and it is our responsibility to protect them.

As parents of preschoolers, we must also be vigilant when our little ones are enjoying time with friends. They need their space to play and learn socialization skills, but we should position ourselves so we can still supervise this interaction. This is especially true in situations where your child is playing with a new friend.

Friendship is like a two-sided coin. We not only want our young children to enjoy good friends, we also want them to *be* good friends. Talk to your child about how to be a friend. Certainly intervene and correct behavior when you see your child is not treating her friends like she would want to be treated. When our daughter was still the only child in the family, she had a tendency to be very bossy. This behavior was most often apparent when she was with her friend, Natalie. She told poor Natalie what she could touch and not touch in *her* toy room and how the permitted toys must be played with. It was shameful to hear our tot ordering around her friend. After the first episode of this kind of behavior was seen, we took swift action and did some serious training. I won't try to tell you it never happened again, but subsequent events involving our three-year-old drill sergeant only required a reminding word or look and pleasantness was restored.

When our little ones enjoy safe and appropriate friendships, they begin to learn how to wisely choose companions for themselves as they grow older. When they learn to be good friends to others, they have the opportunity to be a positive influence for God's Kingdom.

And so I pray…

Jesus, how wonderful it is to call you my friend! I know I can carry everything to you in prayer and you are always there loving me. Guide me in the choices of friends I make for _____. Help me to protect him and choose companions who will influence him for good. Bless my little one with friends who are kind and loving. Shape _____ into a friend who is worthy of loyalty and trust. Encourage him to share with his playmates his child-like understanding of what it means to have a friend in you. Amen.

My Personal Prayer:

How God Answered My Prayer:

Children's Book:

Puppy Makes Friends by Mary Manz Simon

Parenting Resource:

Complete Book of Baby & Child Care: From Pre-Birth through the Teen Years by Dr. Paul Reisser and Dr. James Dobson

Chapter Twenty-Three

TACTICAL ERROR

Praying for Your Little One and Separation Anxiety

Twins, Abby and Elly, had no problem separating from their parents. In fact, even on Saturdays Elly would carry their shoes to the door and Abby would drag their diaper bag, ready to go to daycare. Then they would stand at the door and wave. "Bye-bye, Bye-bye" they would chorus.

At eighteen-months-old, separating from each other was another story. Early one morning Abby woke up and stretched. She looked over at the crib next to hers. Elly was still sleeping. Abby would have to do something about that. She leaned forward and pushed herself up to a standing position, grabbed the rail of her crib, and revved up for an ear shattering beller. Then she let loose. She yelled, cried, shook the crib, and did her best to rouse her curly-headed twin, "Eeeeeeee!"

The girl's mother flew through the door and plucked Miss Abby from her crib. She scooted out of the room and pulled the door behind her, leaving it only slightly ajar. Then she moved into the family room with her darling, but frustrated, bundle. Whew, ugly scene averted. Mom wanted Elly to sleep as long as was necessary for her to wake up in a sweet mood. Hopefully, it would also be long enough for Mom to get a few things done with only one toddler getting into mischief.

Abby, however, was not pleased with her mother's agenda, and she let her know it. Now the cries escalated to genuine wails as she reached for the door behind which her nearly identical twin slept. She wiggled and squirmed in her mother's arms, making every effort to free herself and get to that door. Mom was determined though too, and stronger. Soon Abby was comforted and quieted, and Mom set her down while she went to start breakfast. This was the tactical error Abby had been waiting for. She looked left, then right. Seeing her golden opportunity, with only Mom's bumper showing behind the refrigerator door, Abby made a beeline for her bedroom. She slammed the door open with her little left hand, letting it hit the wall with a crash. She dashed to Elly's crib and poked her fingers between the bars. Grabbing Elly's special blanket, Abby gave a tug and a WHOOP! She was rewarded with a peek and a grin from her first soul mate. Her mother, standing in the doorway, just shook her head.

Do not be anxious about anything,
but in everything by prayer and supplication
with thanksgiving let your requests be made known to God.
Philippians 4:6 (ESV)

Most wee ones go through separation anxiety at some point in their young years. That means most parents can relate to the tears they see streaking down a young mother's face as she listens to the cries of her thirteen-month-old on the other side of the church nursery door. Those hiccuping baby sobs wring our hearts. If you have been there, then you know it doesn't make you feel much better when some well-meaning sort says, "It's okay, honey, this is normal." But, it's true.

Before the age of three, little ones are still learning object permanence. They are figuring out that Mom and Dad are real and will come back for them. The more they are rescued from these situations, the longer it will take them to learn this lesson and master the skill of separation.

Take it from someone who has stood on both sides of the door, this too shall pass.

I have left each of my three children in the nursery and shut the door to their cries. That sounds heartless, but some lessons can't be learned without shedding a few tears. (That's true in the adult years too. I know.) I have also worked in the nursery, babysat for friends and neighbors, and have seen other parents shut the same door, while I held tightly to their screaming child. It gets better.

Crying is normal when it comes to separation, but it is often short lived. Many times the tears are for the benefit of the parent, and once he or she is out of earshot, they turn off as easily as a faucet. Even when the little one does continue crying, she is rewarded with the return of her parent shortly, and the realization that Mom and Dad always return is beginning to take root.

It isn't necessary to apply the "stop, drop, and run" technique when you are leaving your child somewhere, especially in the beginning. If your child is struggling with separation anxiety, there are a number of things you can do to help them master the art of separating. Choose familiar caregivers if possible. When you are getting babysitters, stick with the same one or two, while your child learns to feel safe with these people. If family is available, start by asking them to watch your children, but don't exclusively use family if you can help it. Provide your little one with security items that will help with the transition. Blankets, teddy bears, and even a picture of you can provide comfort for your infant or toddler. Start small and stretch your tot. The first time you may only be able to leave for a few minutes. As you and your child gain confidence and become more secure, you can stretch your separations into longer periods of time. Finally, NEVER SNEAK! Don't sneak away and don't sneak back to check on them. When you leave your child, give them a hug and kiss and assurance, "Mommy is leaving now, but I will be back soon. I love you."

And so I pray…

Dear God, You are faithful to hear my prayers! Thank you for giving me this beautiful child to love and care for. Help me not to smother him now with my presence. I know that he needs to learn that I will always come back for him. Give me the strength to walk away so that he can learn that important lesson. Please put people in

_____'s life with whom he can feel safe and comforted. Help him learn that you are always with him, he is never alone, and Mommy and Daddy will always come back for him. Help him grow to be confident and secure as he walks with you all the days of his life. Amen.

My Personal Prayer:

How God Answered My Prayer:

Children's Book:

Don't Go! by Jane Breskin Zalben

Parenting Resource:

The Parent Survival Guide by Dr. Todd Cartmell

Chapter Twenty-Four
NOW I IS REALLY SCARED
Praying for Your Little One's Sense of Security

My frustration mounted as we pulled into the nearest gas station. We were supposed to be forty miles outside of town in the next ten minutes. There was no way we were going to arrive at our friend's home in time to start making homemade soap before lunch. Every possible obstacle that could have slowed me down that morning did. My three children were unusually quiet in the back of the minivan. I believe they intuitively sensed my growing aggravation and wisely kept to themselves. As I wrote my check for the gas, I realized I didn't know the name of this particular gas station and I grumbled, "I don't have any idea where we are!"

From the seat behind me, I heard my sensitive four-year-old whimper quietly, "Now I is really scared."

Not aware that he had been listening to my self-talk, I turned in my seat and said, "Ben, why would you be scared?"

"'Cuz we is lost," he insisted incredulously.

Still not catching on I said, "Honey, we're not lost. Whatever gave you that idea?"

Ben's eyebrows rose hopefully and he asked, "You mean you know where we is now?!"

I sought the Lord, and he answered me
and he delivered me from all my fears.

Psalm 34:4 (ESV)

When we bring our newborn baby home from the hospital, we are everything to him. When he is hungry, tired, or needs a fresh diaper, he cries and we meet his need. When we meet those needs, our little one learns to trust us. Simply stated, an infant's first experiences in life shape his sense of security.

Sometimes security is found in something tangible that's familiar. Our children each were attached to a stuffed bear that had a blanket for its body. These security friends were carried with them to doctor appointments, the church nursery to help with separation, and on vacations. Some children attach to a pacifier, blanket, or a special doll or stuffed animal. These treasured possessions provide comfort for little ones who are easily afraid.

So many things can cause our preschoolers to question their security in this world. It's even hard to tell the difference between things that are real and things that aren't. Cartoons, fairy tales, and figurative language can be confusing and scary. One of our preschoolers even thought that we hid from "tomatoes" when the tornado sirens sounded their alarm in our neighborhood. They take our words very literally, and sometimes there is a complete misinterpretation of our words.

Our child's fears are very real and they need our comfort and reassurance about those things that cause them concern. We need to remind them that God is faithful, and He is the one they can always look to for their sense of security. He promises never to leave them. God's perfect love can erase all of their fears and they can rest in the security of His arms.

And so I pray...

My Faithful God, What victory we have in the promise you made to deliver us from all our fears! Praise be to you God, who daily renews my faith. Teach me how to share your promises with _____. Fill him with your love and remove any feelings of fear, doubt, or insecurity that he may be experiencing. Father, I pray that you would help me encourage a positive sense of security in my child. Help _____ grow to recognize the difference between things that are real and things that are imaginary so they might not cause him unnecessary fear or concern. Thank you for being in our lives. Because we have you, we never have to accept a spirit of fear and can enjoy a sense of security in you. Amen.

My Personal Prayer:

How God Answered My Prayer:

Children's Book:

Go Away, Dark Night by Liz Curtis Higgs

Parenting Resource:

Complete Book of Baby & Child Care: From Pre-Birth through the Teen Years by Dr. Paul Reisser and Dr. James Dobson

Chapter Twenty-Five
I WANT TO BE JESUS!
Praying for Your Little One and Sibling Rivalry

After spending the weekend at "Camp Grandma and Grandpa," our preschool boys were attempting to "gain the floor" and regale their father with stories from their time at the farm. It didn't take long before they were arguing and demanding equal time and attention from Daddy. Feeling trapped in the minivan and knowing he had another hour to drive with these two, he decided to teach a lesson in brotherly love. "If Jesus were here right now, what would he do?" Neither boy seemed to have any ideas, so he suggested, "I think he would say, 'Let my brother tell you his story first.'" He let them ponder that idea for a minute before he asked, "Who would like to play a game and practice being Jesus?" The boys enthusiastically agreed to try this game.

Feeling quite proud of his strategy for eliminating the sibling squabble, Dad explained that whoever was playing the role of Jesus would let his brother tell about the weekend first. Then they would trade roles. After confirming they both understood the rules of this game, he asked, "Who wants to be Jesus first?" Our youngest son waved his arm in the air and shouted, "ME!" and our older son shared a weekend story. Turn taking continued for a couple of minutes before the coveted role of Jesus became too desirable for the little actors. Fifty-five miles from home Dad was listening to raised voices demanding, "I want to be Jesus," "No, *I* want to be Jesus" bouncing back and forth in the backseat.

Finally, all of you, have unity of mind, sympathy,
brotherly love, a tender heart, and a humble mind.
1 Peter 3:8 (ESV)

Every parent who has more than one child has experienced or will experience sibling rivalry at its best. *"He started it! I had it first! Don't touch me! He's looking at me!"* The only one you might not have heard yet is, *"I get to sit in the front seat!"* and that's only because they are all still strapped in car seats in the back. Whew!

Sibling issues can begin as soon as toddlers are big enough to fight back when their older brother or sister bugs them. Relationships are not easy, especially between young children who lack necessary relationship skills. Sharing and negotiating do not come naturally for preschoolers. Neither do honesty, respect, patience, and problem solving. Instead, our little ones come up swinging, biting, whining, and crying when they feel hurt, angry, or inconvenienced.

As parents, we need to remind our children that their siblings are their best friends. They are going to be a part of each other's lives for the long haul. When we pray at night with our little ones, we should help them lift up their siblings in prayer. Look for opportunities for your children to serve one another. If you are piling in the minivan to run errands, ask the older preschooler to help buckle the younger child. At naptime, when the middle child has lost his precious sleeping companion, encourage all the children to join the search party. Ask the children to help each other with chores, like putting clean socks away and setting the table. At our house, we even have "Team Tiede" cheers that we use to celebrate each other's achievements, which also help promote positive sibling relationships.

When the inevitable happens and you have bickering, step in to teach good communication and problem-solving skills. Sometimes you may have to role-play how one child tells his sister that it "Makes me mad when you take my toy," instead of scratching her face. In other situations, you may model for your child how to read the "whines" of his younger brother and walk away from a situation. At times, it is most effective to separate the squabblers completely. My favorite technique, and my children's least favorite (which is the reason this is so successful), is to implement a "Hug Fest." I turn over our traditional three-minute sand egg timer on the table. Then the siblings stand next to the table and are instructed to gently "hug" until the timer ends. Most of the time this consequence ends in giggles and the offense is forgotten.

Teaching our children to love each other and get along is critical so that "together they may glorify the God and Father of our Lord Jesus Christ, with one heart and mouth" (Romans 15:5-6).

And so I pray...

In Jesus' Name, I pray these things, giving you glory and honor forever, Father! I love my children, and I know they love each other too. Please show me how to encourage _____ in his relationship with his sibling(s). I admit sometimes my first reaction is to step in and stop the fight or raise my own voice louder than those of the children. Help me be a good model of respect and communication for _____. I pray he will learn to live at peace with his sibling(s). Give him the integrity to walk away from situations even if it doesn't mean "winning." Help _____ and his siblings "love one another with brotherly affection. (And) outdo one another in showing honor" (Romans 12:10 ESV). Amen.

My Personal Prayer:

How God Answered My Prayer:

Children's Book:

Brown Bear, White Bear by Svetlana Petrovic

Parenting Resource:

The Parent Survival Guide by Dr. Todd Cartmell

Praying for Your Little One's Behavior

Chapter Twenty-Six
THIS LITTLE PIGGY
Praying for Your Little One's Behavior in Public

Shopping is not my "thing." Let me rephrase that. Shopping WITH CHILDREN is not my thing! Apparently, I have shared my distaste for this practice with my children, as announcing the need for a trip to the store is usually met with a chorus of groans, whines, and whimpers ... even from the two-year-old! The reality is that, more days than not, we have a reason to run to the nearest discount store or supermarket to pick up something essential. One morning my three-year-old climbed onto my bed, where I was still feigning sleep. He asked about our plans for the day and sighed when he heard that we would be making a quick trip to the store. Then he crawled to the end of the bed where my toes peeked out from the covers. The frequency of these errands became obvious to me when he grabbed my big toe between his little fingers and said, "This little piggy goes to Target." The humor of his words weren't lost on me, especially because, in reality, these trips to the store are rarely a laughing matter.

I recall one visit to the grocery store as particularly unpleasant with my young daughter. Kadi fussed incessantly about being confined in her steel prison ... otherwise known as the grocery cart. She became verbally repetitive about wanting to "walk like Mommy!" ("Verbally repetitive" is a kind way of saying she was driving me crazy with her whining and begging!) After eliciting repeated promises to stay by my side and not to touch things, I sprung her from the source of confinement. Kadi looked at the list I had made for her at home. Using pictures I had drawn of her favorite foods (hotdogs, corn, and apple juice), she walked the first aisle at my side, looking for "her" groceries. It wasn't long, however, before she grew bored and began looking for trouble instead. She was tearing up and down the aisles, and rounding the corner, she pulled items off the shelves. After she nearly crashed into a senior citizen, I grabbed my little escape artist and planted her back in the cart. Her wails cinched it. I immediately scanned my list, determined what we absolutely had to have, paid the sympathetic lady at the register, and hurried to the car with my little shopping saboteur.

Wisely realizing that Mommy was one upset woman, my daughter quieted in the car. I took several deep breaths and then turned around in the driver's seat to address my child before pulling out of the parking lot. Deciding to call in the "Big Guy," I said, "Kadi, what do you think Jesus thinks when you act naughty in the store and disobey Mommy?"

"He doesn't like it?" she answered with a questioning tone.

"That's right, young lady." Calming down now, I reminded her of our discussion the night before when we read a story about Jesus dying on the cross for our sins. As we pulled out of the lot, I decided to steer our conversation in this new direction, "Kadi, what do you think Jesus is doing right now in heaven?"

She paused in thought and then, drawing on her own young experience, she replied, "He is listening to me be naughty on his baby monitor."

Even a child makes himself known by his acts,
by whether his conduct is pure and upright.
Proverbs 20:11 (ESV)

I can only imagine that someone is reading this right now and thinking, "I believe I saw that woman and child at the store today!" Perhaps you are even seeing yourself in this situation. It's not pretty, is it? Training children is full-time work. There are days when I drop into bed exhausted from teaching and reteaching the same lessons all day long. When we go into public, whether it's the mall, the grocery store, the park, or church, I hope and pray that my children will remember what I have worked so hard to instill in their hearts and minds. But, alas, it often isn't so.

Perhaps my expectations are too high. Are they bored? Maybe I need to plan distractions for them or age appropriate entertainment to get them through the experience. Are they just excited about all the new things to see and touch? Surely I need to prepare them for the experience by discussing my expectations and establishing rules and limits when free exploration isn't possible for little ones. Most likely I need to readjust my expectations and my plans. Some things that I would like to do and places that I would like to go are simply inappropriate for preschoolers.

And so I pray…

Dear Jesus, I am amazed by your creativity and bountiful provisions! How I delight in watching the wonder in my child's eyes as he sees your world and all that you have blessed us with, for the first time. Forgive me for the times that I am impatient with his need to explore when it isn't convenient for me. Show me how to set appropriate limits for _____ while encouraging his growing appreciation and understanding of your creation. Jesus, please show me how to teach _____ that even as a _____-year-old, he is known by his behavior. Help me to reinforce these behaviors and recognize and celebrate his successes when we are in public and at home! You love _____. Let all that he does be to your glory. Amen.

My Personal Prayer:

How God Answered My Prayer:

Children's Book:

Jingles and Joy by Allison Gappa Bottke and Heather Gemmen

Parenting Resource:

See How They Run by Lorilee Cracker

Chapter Twenty-Seven
NOT A CHOICE
Praying for Your Little One's Obedience

Many families are blessed with at least one drama queen. That's the child who jumps on the fireplace hearth or on a blanket hastily thrown on the floor and has a "stage." Wooden spoons, TV remote controls, and even Barbie dolls are used as makeshift microphones. Our family was blessed with not one drama queen, but a drama queen and two drama kings! Their favorite productions involve recreating Biblical stories.

On one occasion, our eight-year-old daughter was assigned the role of Jesus, her four-year-old brother cast himself as God. 'God' said to 'Jesus', "Come on, Son, it's time to die on the cross now."

'Jesus' emphatically replied, "I don't want to!"

'God's' firm response was, "This is NOT a choice."

Children, obey your parents in everything,
for this pleases the Lord.
Colossians 3:20

Sometimes you are able to give your preschooler choices. "Would you like milk or juice?" "Do you want to wear sandals or your Buzz Lightyear tennis shoes?" In such cases, either choice is acceptable. Other times you are not able to give a choice and the only acceptable response is obedience. Unfortunately, obedience often means doing something that you don't feel like doing at the time. Who wants to do that? It takes an act of obedience for your 18-month-old to leave the baby doll she is pushing in a stroller to have her stinky diaper changed. I used to encourage the right choice by singing, "Hurry, Hurry, run to Mommy! Hurry, Hurry, run to Mommy! Hurry, Hurry, run to Mommy. _____ obeys the first time!" (Sung to the tune of "Hurry, Hurry, Drive the Fire Truck.") Then when my little one ran into my arms, she would be greeted with a huge hug and cheers for her obedience.

The catch with obedience is that it requires willingly submitting to authority. The key word is "willingly." Obedience is a heart issue as we train our children to obey because they are freely choosing to do so, rather than because they are afraid they will get caught and punished if they don't obey.

Obedience means doing what you are told to do without arguing, stalling, or negotiating. When we ask our three-year-old to help us set the table and he says, "In a minute" (I wonder where he heard that? Gulp!), he is being disobedient. When we tell our four-year-old that she needs to get off the computer and get her jammies on and she says, "I just have to finish this ONE game," she is being disobedient. When we have to drive home from the grocery store and our 16-month-old stiffens his body, as we try to maneuver him into his car seat, he is being disobedient.

Our desire is for our children to be obedient because it pleases God. It isn't a choice and there is no greater reason than that.

And so I pray...

My Faithful God, Praise, glory, and honor belong to you.

Sometimes I blow it, and I am not obedient to your will for me and for the way that I parent _____. Merciful God, forgive my own disobedience. Help me to be consistent in my parenting, as I train _____ to obey me. It is the cry of my heart that _____ would learn to obey me so that, in turn, my child would learn to obey you. Show me when it is appropriate to give my little one choices and not be legalistic and when first time obedience to direction is essential. Teach me to be like you; creative and forgiving in my parenting. Thank you, God, for the promise that it will go well with _____ and that he "may live long in the land" if he obeys his parents in the Lord, "for this is right" (Ephesians 6:1-3 ESV). May _____'s life bring glory to you as a result of his obedience to you and to his earthly parents. Amen.

My Personal Prayer:

How God Answered My Prayer:

Children's Book:

Bear Obeys by Dr. Mary Manz Simon

Parenting Book:

Creative Correction: Extraordinary Ideas for Everyday Discipline
by Lisa Welchel

Chapter Twenty-Eight
"MAMA, GET!"
Praying for Your Little One and Temper Tantrums

Two-year-old Abby and her mom were snuggling on the bed one afternoon, enjoying some stories and quiet time together. When Abby got rough with one of the picture books, her mother said they would need to put the books away. Little Miss Abby threw her pacifier on the floor in a fit of rage. Then she screamed in a shrill voice, "Mama, get!"

Abby's mother wasn't about to be told what to do by an unreasonable and unruly little girl. She lowered her voice and said, "No, Abby. You will need to get it yourself."

Abby proceeded to throw a wild tantrum for a full thirty minutes. She kicked, screamed, threw her little body around on the bed, and yelled demands. All the while, her mother sat quietly on the bed, pretending to be peacefully reading James Dobson's book, "The Strong-Willed Child."

After thirty minutes, Abby climbed off the bed. Her mother sighed, believing the tirade was finally over. Abby sat down beside her pacifier on the floor and in a determined voice demanded, "Mama, get!"

A man without self-control is like a city broken into
and left without walls.
Proverbs 25:28 (ESV)

"I must stay calm. Don't scream. Don't crumple to the floor. I am the grownup." These are just a few of the self-talk phrases I have had to use in the middle of a temper tantrum. That is, a temper tantrum thrown by my toddler, and not my own.

The fury of a full-fledged tantrum can be an amazing thing to watch ... in other people's children. But have you noticed that typically your own little ankle-biters save their most extreme emotional outbursts for the most inconvenient moments? That's when you notice everyone else within a city block, stopping to stare in awe. That's not a sympathetic "aaawww" either. You can see judgment in their eyes. I shudder.

So what is the parent of a hissy-fit-throwing preschooler to do? First, try an ounce of prevention. Most little people will start to lose it when they are tired, hungry, over-stimulated, struggling with a transition, or keeping an unrealistic schedule. Do everything in your power to eliminate or control these triggers. Second, when you recognize that your preschooler is exercising some serious self-control in a situation that might otherwise end in a tantrum, praise him with words of affirmation and encouragement.

When the inevitable happens and your preschooler loses control and flies into a raging tantrum; stop, drop, and roll. No, I'm kidding, although it might shock your toddler into stopping the temper tantrum. Really, what you need to do is make sure your child is safe and then leave the area immediately. I am talking IMMEDIATELY. Do not engage this little tornado in any conversation. Simply remove the audience. Yep. It's a show all right and it is for your benefit. When you are out of sight and not interacting with your drama king or queen, he or she will likely allow their rage to fizzle out. If you have a really determined tantrum thrower who figures out this strategy and starts to follow you around with his tantrum, then quickly move him to your predetermined Time Out spot and let your preschooler calm down in a safe and boring place.

Temper tantrums demonstrate a lack of self-control. As parents, if we don't reward such behavior with attention, it will stop. No one likes to deal with adults who yell, stomp their foot, and throw themselves around a room when they don't get their way. Deal with your preschooler's tantrums now so that his behavior may be pleasing to others and glorifying to God.

And so I pray…

Patient God, Thank you for loving my children even when they are driving me crazy. You are awesome! Thank you for providing your son, Jesus, as a model of how we should exercise self-control in our lives. I pray that _____'s walk will be blameless. Help him to control his temper and to demonstrate feelings appropriately. Teach _____ your ways and renew a right spirit within him. May _____ bear fruit of the Spirit; love, joy, peace, patience, kindness, goodness, faithfulness, gentleness, and self-control (Galatians 5:22-23). Amen.

My Personal Prayer:

How God Answered My Prayer:

Children's Book:

Tristan's Temper Tantrum by Caroline Formby

Parenting Resource:

See How They Run by Lorilee Craker

Chapter Twenty-Nine
NO, NO, GRANDMA!
Praying for Your Little One's Time Out

When my daughter was only weeks past her second birthday, Grandma came to visit. Shortly after her arrival, we were all seated on the living-room floor playing together. Interspersed with our play, which was directed by our two-year-old CEO, my mother and I exchanged stories and friendly banter. I don't recall exactly what clever thing I must have said, but my mother playfully smacked me on the leg. My daughter gasped in horror! "No, no, Grandma! Don't hit Mommy!"

My mother and I exchanged looks and stifled giggles behind our hands. Grandma had no time to explain her behavior before Kadi announced, "You need a Time Out on the steps!" (Our little micro-manager had some personal experience with Time Outs on the steps. It was much less fun than her bedroom.) Grandma obediently went to the steps, followed by Kadi. After Grandma settled herself on the bottom step Kadi, marched in front of her, assumed the "hands-on-hips" stance, and demanded, "Now tell me what happened here!"

> *Listen to advice and accept instruction,*
> *that you may gain wisdom in the future.*
> Proverbs 19:20

Time Outs are seldom easy and not much fun. That's the way they are supposed to be. If our little ones enjoyed Time Out it wouldn't serve as an effective negative consequence for their bad behavior. But no one ever told me it would be hard for me too. Sometimes dealing with Time Outs makes me want to cry myself! If I'm not handling Time Out effectively, then my preschooler leaves his assigned spot, and I have to haul him back again and again. My ears ring with the shrill protests of his discontent. It's then that I sometimes put myself in Mommy Time Out and hide in the bathroom. If only the rule applied to adults that the number of minutes we earn in Time Out should equal our age! (Sigh.)

Having a plan to handle Time Outs and sticking to that plan are the keys to effective Time Outs. When the time calls for it, I immediately need to escort my preschooler to a safe and boring place where he can spend a few minutes and I can monitor his actions. I need to praise my little guy when he successfully serves his time and changes his behavior. Most important, I need to erase any sense of guilt from my conscience for enforcing appropriate and necessary Time Outs.

When my hands form the shape of a "T," in the familiar basketball signal for Time Out, I need to remember that shaping my child's heart is my most important responsibility as a parent. I want my little one to learn to quiet himself in Time Out so that he can learn to recognize another familiar "t" shape, that of the cross. I am being obedient to my own Father when I "train up (my) child in the way he should go, (so that) even when he is old he will not depart from it" (Proverbs 22:6).

And so I pray…

My Patient God, Teach me your ways. I admit sometimes I try to parent on my own. I depend on my own resources, strength and wisdom. Forgive me. I need your direction. Time Outs are difficult for

_____. God, help me handle these situations with your patience

and mercy. Help me be firm with _____ just as you are firm with

me when I step out of your will. Please place your hand over my mouth

when I am tempted to raise my voice or say something that may hurt

_____'s spirit. Shape _____'s heart so that it is pleasing to

you. Guide her development so that she can be weaned from Time Outs

entirely. Thank you for taking time out just for me as you have

promised to be with me always in my parenting. Amen.

My Personal Prayer:

How God Answered My Prayer:

Children's Book:

   Dinofours: It's Time-Out Time by Steve Metzger

Parenting Resource:

   Creative Correction: Extraordinary Ideas for Everyday Discipline by Lisa Whelchel

Chapter Thirty
CAN YOU HEAR ME NOW?
Praying for Your Little One's Whining

Cell phones have been a serious source of frustration for me. It seems as though what makes life easier for others is my handicap. Perhaps it's because I am technologically challenged or maybe it's because there used to be a lack of cell phone towers in the area I live. Regardless of the reason, my children have often heard me mimic a well-known line from an old cell phone commercial, "Can you hear me now?"

My second frustration with cell phones actually applies to all telephones. Whenever I put a phone to my ear, I hear this terrible whining noise. It doesn't matter how much I tap on the phone, switch channels, or change positions, the whining continues. That's when I become aware of the fact that the whining isn't coming from the receiver, but rather from the "ankle-biters" who are hanging around my feet. Sometimes the annoying whine continues even after I hang up the phone.

I never cease to be surprised that my normally verbose preschooler, who has an extensive vocabulary, can get stuck on one word for five minutes or repeat the same request a bazillion times. "Mom, Mom, Mom, MOMmy, MomMEEEEE!" It's not even the repetition that drives me batty, but the pitch that my preschooler is able to produce!

One day after exhausting the demand, "I waanntt some candy!' twenty times to no avail, my two year old disappeared. Whew! A Mommy reprieve! I was celebrating my apparent victory. Obviously my strategy of telling him that Mommy couldn't hear him when he used that whining voice, had finally paid off. Just then he came back in to me and stood at my side. He pulled a little red toy cell phone out of his pocket, flipped it open, expertly put it up to his ear and asked, "Can you hear me NOW? I WANT SOME CANDY!"

Do all things without grumbling or disputing, that you may be
blameless and innocent, children of God without blemish
in the midst of a crooked and twisted generation,
among whom you shine as lights in the world.
Philippians 2:14-15 (ESV)

Whining can make the most patient parent "lose it." Sometimes it seems as though every limit I set is met with whining. I hate to admit it, but sometimes it works for them. I am worn out and worn down by their incessant complaining, and I let them have whatever they are requesting, to gain a little peace for myself. Almost without failure, every time I give in, I regret it. The only thing I really gained is the promise of more whining, because now my preschooler has learned it works!

When we set limits with our children and they whine in response, they are being disobedient. It's really that simple. I have given an answer or made a request that didn't fit in with the plans my child had for himself, and he chooses to demonstrate his frustration by whining.

Am I really that different? When God points me in a direction or answers my prayers in ways I hadn't counted on, don't I stomp my feet like a two year old and think, "He can't mean it! 'Reconsider, God, please, please, please!'" Does that sound all too familiar? Whining to God doesn't change our circumstances anymore than our children's whining should change their circumstances or our decisions. Taking the time to break our children of the whining habit will serve them well in the future. When, in the course of their life, God gives your child an answer that he hadn't planned, he will graciously be able to respond by saying, "Then show me your will and your way, Father."

And so I pray...

Merciful God, You are faithful to hear all our prayers! I praise you for giving us voices with which we can bring our needs and desires to you. Forgive me for complaining when I don't appreciate all that you do for me. Help me set a good example for _____ by not whining to you, to my spouse, and to my child. Give me the endurance to stick to my guns, even when my child is persisting in his demands. Show me how to teach _____ appropriate and acceptable ways to communicate with those in authority so that he may also talk to you respectfully. May _____'s words always be music to your ears. Amen.

My Personal Prayer:

How God Answered My Prayer:

Children's Book:

Sophie and Sam: When to Say "Yes" and When to Say "No" by Tori Cloud

*This book also has stories covering; honesty, sharing, respect, clean-up, meanies, following rules, manners, arguing, and thanking God. Highly Recommended!

Parenting Resource:

First-Time Mom by Dr. Kevin Leman

Chapter Thirty-One

TWENTY LITTLE TOES

Praying for Your Little One and Accepting Limits

Deborah, five, and Elizabeth, three, were supposed to be helping Mom with some weekly house cleaning one sunny summer morning. Instead of helping however, they seemed to be creating more mess in the dining room, living room, and playroom. Frustrated with the progress she wasn't making, their mother, Ann, sent the girls outside to play near the front door with a favorite toy.

It wasn't long before the girls marched back in the house with dandelion bouquets for Mom. Up the stairs they came, around the corner and right through the pile of crumbs on her freshly swept kitchen floor, to present her with these gifts. Mom did not receive her gifts with much grace. Instead she instructed, "You two girls get out of this kitchen RIGHT NOW! In fact, here is the 'do not pass' line," she ordered, pointing toward the metal strip that separated the carpeting in the living room from the entrance to the kitchen. "I do not want to see you on this side of the line. Do you understand me?"

The girls nodded, not too concerned with their mom's cranky demeanor, and scampered off to their "secret" corner of the living room to discuss their next plan. This was the first time Ann had seen her daughters showing any type of teamwork or sisterhood without bickering. While she was still frustrated with the condition of her home and the constant interruptions, she returned to the chore of sweeping up the scattered pile of crumbs, thrilled to see them working nicely together. Just as Ann finished sweeping, the girls caught her attention.

Deborah and Elizabeth had approached the "do not pass" line. Their twenty little toes were just a hair's breadth from falling into the forbidden zone, but so far they had accepted the limit she had so dictated. Ann was just about to warn them of their impending doom should they cross that line when she heard a sound that melted her crabby heart. "Jesus Loves Me, this I know ..." they sweetly sang. What was a mother to do? She gathered her little lambs in her arms and asked for their forgiveness. As she did so she was reminded that it was all about control. The girls had self-control when they toed the line, and God was in control even when her life with little ones seemed as messy as scattered crumbs on a kitchen floor.

For the moment all discipline seems painful rather than pleasant, but later it yields the peaceful fruit of righteousness to those who have been trained by it.
Hebrews 12:11 (ESV)

"No." It usually makes most kids' top ten word lists. They learn it early and use it often. Yet, when they hear grownups, particularly parents, direct the word to them, they look appalled. "No? Did you just say 'No' to me? Are you serious? You can't mean 'NO!'"

"Toddlers are perverse creatures, capricious and whimsical," says *See How They Run* author, Lori Craker. "They can come completely unglued by the word *no*. A toddler finds the frustration of being denied what seems to be a perfectly reasonable request as painful as running into a brick wall."

Having limits set on a preschooler's independence is both necessary and yet completely frustrating to these little explorers. They are ready to test the boundaries and discover their worlds. Giving little ones reasonable freedoms, with their safety assured, can lessen their frustration with limits. When we provide our children with safe places to explore their environments, they gain both competence and confidence.

If you can say "no" without saying "no," do so. (Don't roll your eyes, this will make sense. Stick with me.) When you find creative ways to redirect, distract, or offer another acceptable option to your preschooler, rather than telling him "no" for the umpteenth time, he will be much more accepting of limits. If your sixteen-month-old is eating crackers in her highchair, and you know she has nearly reached her limit, set two more crackers on the table next to the tray. Beside the crackers set a book, bubbles, or another enticing toy. Then explain, "You may have two more crackers. They are right here when you are ready for them. When these are gone we are going to blow some bubbles!" There you go. You have set a limit, without saying "no," and you have offered both a distraction and an acceptable option. Every time you catch your little peanut accepting "no" without a meltdown, praise her socks off!

All of our lives we are faced with boundaries, limits, and that two letter N-O. If our little ones learn to accept limits now, they will be equipped and prepared to submit to the authority that is placed over them for their protection for the rest of their lives. Jesus blesses those who submit to authority.

And so I pray…

Dear Jesus, You are all-knowing and compassionate. I praise you for you know when I need to set limits with my little one, and you understand his frustration with those same limits. Don't let me exasperate _____ with unnecessary limits; instead help me bring him up in the discipline and instruction of your Word (Ephesians 6:4). Guide me as I determine limits that are necessary for _____'s safety and well-being. Teach my little one to obey me in everything, for this pleases you (Colossians 3:20). Amen.

My Personal Prayer:

How God Answered My Prayer:

Children's Book:

Mommy, May I Hug the Fishes? by Crystal Bowman

Parenting Resource:

First-Time Mom by Dr. Kevin Leman

Chapter Thirty-Two
JUST MY TEETH
Praying for Your Little One and Aggression

Our two- and four-year-old sons share bunk beds. Sleeping with a four-foot space between them is a good thing. The only time, in fact, they are allowed to sleep together is when we visit Grandma and Grandpa at the farm. For the most part these two love each other and get along grand. Little Caleb lives to follow around his big brother, Ben, and Ben relishes bossing and harassing Caleb. The problem is Ben doesn't always intuitively know when to stop, and Caleb doesn't always choose to use his language to tell him to stop. This is where the problems start when they share a bed.

One spring evening we were visiting family for the weekend, and the boys had been tucked in the double bed in the basement. Kisses were exchanged, prayers shared, and promises of serious consequences were made should they play instead of sleep. Then the grownups went upstairs to do what grownups do after little children are in bed; eat and play card games.

Things were quiet for a while … perhaps too quiet. Then we heard it. We knew immediately what had happened. We had only heard this sound a handful of times in the last year, but it was unmistakable. Ben's hysterical screaming could only mean one thing. Caleb had bitten him.

We flew down the stairs and met Ben as he made his escape from the bedroom into the family room. He crawled onto my lap and sobbed into my shoulder as I surveyed the damage. Eight little teeth marks formed a perfect circle on his lower back. Before I could even offer words of comfort, Caleb made his way into the family room, also wailing. "He hit me!" he cried.

"Only after he started it" inserted an indignant Ben. Then the wailing escalated from both boys.

A few minutes passed, and we started the inquisition. Ben confessed he had indeed hit Caleb, but the boy to whom the teeth marks belonged refused to admit any wrongdoing. "Did you bite your brother; yes or no?" I asked him point blank.

Caleb sighed, puffed out his chest, looked me in the eye, and said, "I touched his back."

"With what?" I probed.

"Just my teeth." That was his final answer.

Be angry and do not sin.

Ephesians 4:26 (ESV)

Aggression is seldom a pretty scene. As parents, we shrivel inside when we see or hear that our precious little one has acted aggressively, whether he has used his hands, feet, or teeth. Why does this happen? It's not like we go around biting our children and they learn that little trick from us!

Biting is a bit unique in that some children don't bite to be aggressive. Some little ones bite when they become overexcited or are really happy. That may sound odd, but it's true. My husband was carrying our three-year-old (the biter) upside-down. Caleb and Daddy were laughing hysterically one minute, and the next, Daddy was yelling and Caleb was crying. In his excitement, Caleb took a bite out of

Daddy. It wasn't premeditated. It seldom is. In fact, I think after the fact, biters often wonder what just happened.

Biting or demonstrating other forms of aggression often happen when preschoolers are feeling angry, frustrated, or jealous. When they have little or no control over the world around them, aggression often seems like the best solution, especially when their communication skills are lacking. Teaching children under the age of three to use baby sign language can reduce much of the frustration associated with this age group and can improve their ability to express feelings with words rather than aggression. Baby signs allow children to bypass spoken language for the time being and get on with communication.

Help your young children develop a plan for those times when they are feeling especially angry or frustrated. Teach them to walk away from such situations, ask their playmate to stop whatever behavior they are finding offensive, or find Mom and Dad for help. Always praise your preschooler when you catch her expressing anger in a healthy and acceptable manner.

Anger is a natural feeling, and God's Word doesn't tell us to avoid it. We need to teach our preschooler that the Bible tells us not to sin when we are angry. Demonstrating self-control when they are angry is pleasing to God.

And so I pray…

My Jesus, You are the God of Peace. Thank you for modeling the behavior I, myself, need to model for my little one. Help me control my own anger and frustration so my preschooler knows what is acceptable and right. Teach _____ to be "quick to hear, slow to speak, slow to anger, for the anger of man does not produce the righteousness of

God (James 1:19-20). Please lay your hand on _____'s shoulder and stop him when he is about to express his anger, frustration, over-excitement, and even happiness inappropriately. Let him be self-controlled and display integrity. Amen.

My Personal Prayer:

How God Answered My Prayer:

Children's Book:

Mad Maddie Maxwell by Stacie Maslyn

Parenting Resource:

Lifelines: Survival Tips for Parents of Preschoolers by Becky Freeman

Praying for Your Little One's Spiritual Growth & Salvation

Chapter Thirty-Three
GIFT OF GRACE
Praying for Your Little One's
Spiritual Growth & Salvation

Jon sat on the wooden church pew with his four-year-old legs dangling several inches above the floor. On a typical Sunday he was distracted by his six siblings sitting around him. This Sunday was different. Pastor was sharing about the "wages of sin" and the eternal price one would pay if his sins were not forgiven. Jon heard the pastor say that when someone died, the price for unforgiven sin would be to stand before Jesus and hear Him say, "depart from me, I never knew you."

Jon's dad read from the Bible after every meal, so he had heard all of this before, but never had the words captivated him like this morning. Oblivious to the world around him, Jon's heart was beating faster as he listened to the pastor. "God sent Jesus, to pay for our sins for us. He died on the cross and rose again from the dead. We accept that gift when we believe and accept Him as our Savior and Lord."

Sitting in that pew, with the sun shining in through the windows, it dawned on Jon that he was a sinner. He lied to his parents and was sometimes mean to his brothers and sisters. He was afraid if he died, Jesus would tell him to "depart," and he would not spend eternity with Jesus, whom he had grown to love. He didn't want that to happen!

The next morning Jon's feet crunched on the gravel as he made his way to the barn where his dad was cleaning the calf pens. Jon hurried into the barn through a side door and made his way to the pen his dad was cleaning. Along the inside wall was a hay manger from which the calves ate. Jon climbed into it.

"Hi, Jonty! Did you need something?"

"I want to be saved. Can you help me?"

Jon's dad leaned his pitchfork against the wall and climbed into the manger with his son. Together they talked about what it means to be saved. Assured that his young son understood, his father instructed, "Jonty, just tell Jesus what is in your heart."

Kneeling in the fresh straw with his little hands folded and resting on top of the manger, Jon prayed, "Dear Jesus, I know I am a sinner. Please forgive me. Come into my heart and live forever. Amen." Then Jon turned to peek at his father. He wondered if he had said the right words.

His dad cleared his throat and swiped his eyes. He held his son close. Young Jon had a deep desire to share the good news. He jumped down from the manger and headed for the house – he wanted to tell his mom he'd asked Jesus into his heart. He ran toward the house excited about his new gift – grace.

> *We are children of God, and if children, then heirs –*
> *heirs of God and fellow heirs with Christ,*
> *provided we suffer with him*
> *in order that we may also be glorified with him.*
> Romans 8:16-17 (ESV)

Is there any greater gift that you can ever give your child than eternal life? I once heard that most people would never consider entering a burning building if they knew it was empty. However, if they knew for certain that there was a baby inside; they wouldn't hesitate for a second to enter the building to try to save the baby. I'm not suggesting something that would make firefighters send me nasty letters here. I am saying that our instinct would be to save the baby. The souls of our little ones are precious and no matter what pain our prayers may cost us, the reward of eternal life for our child is worth it.

You must never underestimate the power of a parent's prayers. I don't believe anyone comes to know Jesus, unless someone is praying for them. If you don't pray for your child to have a personal relationship with Jesus, who will pray? No one is better equipped to pray for your little one than you are. No one knows him as intimately as you do. Because of the genuine love you have for your preschooler, you are uniquely qualified to come to Jesus with your urgent requests about his needs and problems.

Your child is a precious gift from God to you as a parent. He is already involved in the life of your little one. When you are praying for the salvation of your child, you are praying in one accord with God. Jesus said, *"Let the little children come to me and do not hinder them, for to such belongs the kingdom of heaven"* (Matthew 19:14). You can't go wrong. You also can't make the decision *for* your child.

You do not get to give the gift of grace to your preschooler. The best you can do is accept the gift yourself. Then you must pray without ceasing for your little one. Enlist specific prayer warriors for your child, such as family and friends who also love him, and are willing to receive prayer updates from time to time. You can tell your child stories about Jesus, sing songs to him about his love, and let him see you spending time in prayer and study. You take him to church where he can meet and learn from others who know Jesus, and pray for your little one some more. Only God can give your child salvation.

God has his own timing and your little one may not accept Jesus as his Savior for many years. Praying for your little one's salvation requires patience, perseverance, and faith. Just because your little one isn't even old enough to talk, and couldn't possibly accept Jesus yet, doesn't mean you should wait to pray. Start now! God hears the urgency of a parent's prayers. Don't give up. When you demonstrate your own commitment to Jesus and spend time with Him in prayer, your preschooler may follow your example. Jesus is waiting for him to ask for the gift of grace himself.

And so I pray…

Dear Jesus, What joy it is to have received your gift of grace. Words aren't enough to thank you for being my Savior. Being a parent is a high calling, and I don't always feel worthy. Shape me into a parent who shares my faith with my preschooler through my words and actions. Please put people in _____ 's life who will also gently instruct him in your Word and your ways. I pray that when he grows older, _____ may receive forgiveness of sins and enjoy the gift of salvation. Please draw my son to you, so that he may be a joint heir with you and share in your glory for eternity. Amen

My Personal Prayer:

How God Answered My Prayer:

Children's Book:

If Jesus Lived Inside My Heart by Jill Roman Lord

Parenting Resource:

Complete Book of Baby & Child Care: From Pre-Birth through the Teen Years by Dr. Paul Reisser and Dr. James Dobson

Recommended Children's Books

Character

Perseverance:

>*Keep Trying Travis* by Happy Day Book

Wisdom:

>*God's Wisdom for Little Girls* by Elizabeth George

>*God's Wisdom for Little Boys* by Jim George

Patience:

>*Remy the Rhino Learns Patient* by Andy McGuire

Self-Control:

>*Play with Me* by Marie Hall Ets

Responsibility:

>*Zachary's Zoo* by Mike and Amy Nappa

Respect Authority:

>*Don't Do that Dexter* by Happy Day Book

Honesty:

>*Piglet Tells the Truth* by Mary Manz Simon

Conscience:

>*Right Choices* by Kenneth Taylor

Development

Health:

>*Bear Feels Sick* by Karma Wilson

Potty Training:

>*My Big Boy Undies* and *My Big Girl Undies* by Karen Katz

Bedtime:

    Bed Time Blessings by Dandi Daley Mackall

    Cleaning Up Toys: *Let's Be Helpful* by P.K. Hallinan

Speech and Language:

    God, I Need to Talk to you about Bad Words by Susan K. Leigh

Safety:

    Percy Plays It Safe by Stuart J. Murphy

Morning Routines:

    Sophie and Sam: When to Say "Yes" and When to Say "No" by Tori Cloud

Social Skills

Manners:

    Panda is Polite by Dr. Mary Manz Simon

Mealtimes:

    I Don't Like It by Heather Gemmen

Sharing:

    Lion Can Share by Dr. Mary Manz Simon

Tattling:

    The Tattletale by Lynn Downey

Friends:

    Puppy Makes Friends by Mary Manz Simon

Separation Anxiety:

    Don't Go! by Jane Breskin Zalben

Security:

    Go Away, Dark Night by Liz Curtis Higgs

Sibling Rivalry:

    Brown Bear, White Bear by Svetlana Petrovic

Behavior

Public Behavior:

> *Jingles and Joy* by Allison Gappa Bottke and Heather Gemmen

Obedience:

> *Bear Obeys* by Dr. Mary Manz Simon

Temper Tantrums:

> *Tristan's Temper Tantrum* by Caroline Formby

Time Out:

> *Dinofours: It's Time-Out Time* by Steve Metzger

Whining:

> *Sophie and Sam: When to Say "Yes" and When to Say "No"* by Tori Cloud

Accepting Limits:

> *Mommy, May I Hug the Fishes?* by Crystal Bowman

Aggression:

> *Mad Maddie Maxwell* by Stacie Maslyn

Spiritual Growth and Salvation

Salvation:

> *If Jesus Lived Inside My Heart* by Jill Roman Lord

Recommended Parenting Resources

Complete Book of Baby & Child Care: From Pre-Birth through the Teen Years by Dr. Paul Reisser and Dr. James Dobson (Colorado Springs: Focus on the Family, 2007).

For:

> Perseverance
>
> Honesty
>
> Health
>
> Safety
>
> Friends
>
> Security
>
> Spiritual Growth and Security

Creative Correction: Extraordinary Ideas for Everyday Discipline by Lisa Welchel (Colorado Springs: Focus on the Family, 2005).

For:

> Patience
>
> Tattling
>
> Obedience
>
> Time Out

First-Time Mom by Dr. Kevin Leman (Wheaton, IL: Tyndale, 2004).

For:

> Morning Routines
>
> Whining
>
> Accepting Limits

Lifelines: Survival Tips for Parents of Preschoolers by Becky Freeman
(Wheaton, IL: Tyndale, 2003).

For:

      Potty Training

      Bedtime

      Mealtimes

      Aggression

Don't Make me Count to Three by Ginger Plowman (Wapwallopen,
PA: Shepherd Press, 2003).

For:

      Self-Control

      Responsibility

      Respect Authority

      Sharing

      Wisdom

      Conscience

      Manners

The Parenting Survival Guide by Dr. Todd Cartmell (Grand Rapids,
MI: Zondervan, 2001).

For:

      Cleaning Up Toys

      Separation Anxiety

      Sibling Rivalry

See How They Run: An Energizing Guide to Keep Up with Your Turbo Toddler by Lorilee Craker (Colorado Springs: Waterbrook Press, 2004).

For:

Speech and Language

Public Behavior

Temper Tantrums

The Mommy Manual: Planting Roots that Give Your Children Wings by Barbara Curtis (Create Space, 2010).

Shepherding a Child's Heart by Tedd Tripp (Wapwallopen, PA: Shepherd Press, 1995).

About the Author

Vicki Tiede is an inspiring Bible teacher, conference speaker, and author. Her passion is to open the Scriptures with women in order to share God's grace and enduring faithfulness. Vicki transparently relates life experiences that resonate and draw others into a lifelong pursuit of knowing God.

Living in Rochester, Minnesota, Vicki is a wife, homeschooling mom, and the coordinator of women's ministries in her local church. Vicki holds master's degrees in Ministry and in Education.

Vicki is the author of:

> *Parenting On Your Knees: The Preschool Years*
> *When Your Husband is Addicted to Pornography ... Healing*
> *Your Wounded Heart* (2012)
> *Plug Me In and Let Me Charge Overnight* (2009)

Vicki is also a contributing author for five books.

Visit Vicki on the Web at:

www.VickiTiede.com

Look for other books

published by

www.PixNPens.com

and

www.WriteIntegrity.com

Made in the USA
San Bernardino, CA
20 September 2016